Giuseppe Marinoni
Giovanni Chiaramonte

# THE EVOLVING EUROPEAN CITY

*Translated by Joyce Myerson*

McGill-Queen's University Press
Montreal & Kingston · London · Ithaca

©2014 Ultreya, Milano
All rights reserved

English translation © McGill-Queen's University Press 2015

ISBN 978-0-7735-4528-1


Legal deposit second quarter 2015
Bibliothèque nationale du Québec


Project originated by Giuseppe Marinoni
Maps by StudioMarinoni
Design: Vilma Cernikyte

Printed in Italy

The translation of this work has been funded by SEPS
Segretariato Europeo per le Pubblicazioni Scientifiche
Via Val d'Aposa 7 – 40123 Bologna – Italy
seps@seps.it – www.seps.it

McGill-Queen's University Press acknowledges the support of the Canada Council for the Arts for our publishing program. We also acknowledge the financial support of the Government of Canada through the Canada Book Fund for our publishing activities.



Library and Archives Canada Cataloguing in Publication

Marinoni, Giuseppe, 1961-
[Città europea in evoluzione. English]
The evolving European city / Giuseppe Marinoni, Giovanni Chiaramonte.

Translation of: Città europea in evoluzione.
Includes bibliographical references.
Translated from the Italian.

ISBN 978-0-7735-4528-1 (pbk.)

1. City planning - Europe - Case studies.
2. City planning - Europe - Pictorial works.
I. Chiaramonte, Giovanni, 1948 -, photographer
II. Title. II. Title: Città europea in evoluzione. English.

HT169.E8M3713 2015      307.1'216094      C2014-907337-2

Contents

8 Introduction

15 **Almere**, Stadshart

33 **Amsterdam**, Borneo Sporenburg, Oostelijk Havengebied

55 **Amsterdam**, Zuidas

73 **Barcelona**, Vila Olimpica, Forum 2004

93 **Berlin**, Potsdamer Platz

109 **Breda**, Chassé Park

127 **Hamburg**, HafenCity

147 **Lille**, Euralille

163 **Lisbon**, Expo98, Gare do Oriente, Parque do Tejo

181 **London**, Canary Wharf

199 **Milan**, Grande Bicocca

215 **Milan**, Nuova Portello

231 **Paris**, Parc Bercy, Seine Rive Gauche

253 **Saint-Denis**, Plaine Saint-Denis

270 Bibliography

# Introduction

This book is an exploration of the continually changing and developing universe of urban planning practices – a set of approaches, methods, and theoretical and design tools that is changing the European city. Unlike the 1960s, which were oriented towards deriving urban and territorial architectures from the policies of economic programming, and unlike the 1970s, which were interested in devising general theories relating to "the critical reconstruction" of the city, design disciplines since the mid-1980s formulate methods of urban renewal during operations and confront, as they occur, the conflicts generated by the incessant pressures of changing contemporary economic, social, and technical needs.

The building of large and complex city sections, like those presented in this volume, is the main concern of urban development planning. And although it is an imperfect, contradictory, and constantly evolving tool, urban development planning remains one of the few practicable ways to operate within an ongoing process and within a separateness of times, means, disciplines, and skills, while aiming to contribute to an increase in the quality of urban life.

Urban planning represents a probing into the reality of the evolving European city and produces multiple and perfectible methods for revitalization, formulated concretely and specifically in terms of cases, circumstances, and emergencies. What emerges is a pluralistic horizon, with piecemeal and eclectic approaches, through which a common European profile of urban transformation shines, respectful of the essence, values, and customs of the existing city, aware of operating within the conflicts induced by the processes of innovation and adaptation of the city itself, processes necessary for its protection and survival.

In the sharing of the values expressed by the "compact city," the new urban areas explored in this book express a concentration of functions and themes, a morphological and social pluralism, a co-existence of building, landscape, and infrastructure features, an adherence to the principles of environmental sustainability, and an urban structure stability in housing dynamics. And they distance themselves from both the imitative and conservative mindsets of the historic city and the enthusiastic visions still glimpsed in the urban sprawl, the settlement model most suited to the present day.

Contemporary varied practices of urban planning, which include skills and techniques for strategic action within cities, are rooted in the theoretical and critical contribution of research on the historical European city conducted in the 1960s, the partial critical reconstruction experiments on European cities in the 1970s, and the special projects promoted in the 1980s as a reaction to the contradictory effects of the metropolitan phenomenon.

While urban reconstruction in the 1970s was sustained by the myths of *Kleinstadt* and faith in the "conventions" of the city of the past, today's approaches to urban planning reveal elements of openness and renewal of the existing city, starting precisely from the comparison with the tensions emerging from the contemporary metropolitan situation. The necessary synthesis of housing and infrastructure, the process of including landscape and geography into the existing city, the appeals for sustainability of urban growth, the emerging practices of demolition and reconstruction and of infill (land-recycling) constitute a pretext for the renewal and emancipation of collective traditions, of the functions and forms of the traditional city, no longer under threat of annihilation.

This identification of practices, plans, and implementations since the 1990s in the cities of Europe allows us to define the admittedly unstable boundaries of a field that, while continuously evolving in terms of approaches and methods, operates, often empirically, within extremely dynamic contexts. Energy is drawn precisely from the current unstable situation of economic, social, and epistemological upheavals, energy capable of configuring new quality urban spaces that arise by breaking tired old customs, dodging routine procedures, and destabilizing conventions within the disciplines.

The "metamorphosis of urban design" (Marinoni 2005) has been much talked about. The concept refers to the multiple and multi-faceted consequences that concern the changes in the ways in which one looks and studies the city and the changes in the building processes of the city itself, which, in the transition from "historic European city" to "contemporary city," has been hit by the volatility of ongoing urban phenomena. The new criteria for intervening and interacting with the conflicts of the contemporary city have, above all, produced a rupture of the already unstable boundaries of the urban disciplines. Architecture, town planning, landscape designing, and infrastructure designing have, in fact, seen their respective certainties dissolved. These principles had been patiently conceived in an effort to reconstitute the disciplines, launched, on the one hand, by taking leave of the "modern city," or, on the other, by determinedly following the social and urban reform proposal triggered by the idea of modernity.

A discomfort and an uncertainty in the designing of the contemporary city bring us to reflect upon the profound changes that have unsettled both city and society during the early twenty-first century. The great crisis, which occurred in the 1970s and 1980s, opened a definite post-Ford phase by Harvey (1990), a post-urban phase by Hall (1973), a postmodern phase by Lyotard (1979) and by Jameson (1984), and brought to light new aspects inherent in the urban, human, and social condition and in the contradictions of the contemporary city.

First and foremost, the city has changed – and not according to the predictions and expectations of the urban disciplines. Since the 1960s, the study of the past has failed to appreciate the fact that the city itself comprised a smaller percentage of buildings. In relation to political-economic strategies, rational-comprehensive approaches were formulated to regulate urban and territorial development. But the cities were overwhelmed by phenomena of urbanization, which have quickly and uncontrollably produced the largest metropolitan conurbations. Today we are more aware of the dangers inherent in such vertiginous instability. And we distance ourselves from the limitless illuminist faith in the rational control of urban and territorial transformation that fed the enthusiasms of the International Congress of Modern Architecture (CIAM) and the systemic approaches of the 1960s.

We are also aware of our diminished ability to fully describe ongoing urban phenomena. The "urban condition" provokes disorientation in its inhabitants and a sense of impotence in the scholars that ready themselves to describe its wide-ranging phenomenology. The crisis in the representation of the metropolis in traditional terms invalidates the approach of morphological analyses and the descriptive models of the urban sciences; it frustrates them as tools of investigation and comprehension and as preliminaries to action.

If it is more and more difficult to understand what is happening in the city by means of urban disciplines, it is necessary to widen the field to other inputs. It seems that it may be more suitable to speak of "levels of reality" and "theme maps" (Piattelli Palmarini 1987), multiple and oblique transitory readings of contemporary conditions in both city and society, a palimpsest of figures of speech to describe the city, which, as a whole, escapes definition. And then we also turn to the narrative and interpretive views of photography, film, and literature from which we wish to derive understanding in order to identify the elusive features of the variegated metropolitan phenomenon.

*The Coordinated Urban Plan*
Coordinated urban planning, as it is configured in the more successful examples illustrated in this book, reaches its objective upon the completion of broad parts of a city, in a relatively short time span, with respect to the centuries-long timeframes for the building of the city. The different building, infrastructure, and landscape components are coordinated by a planner, so that together these elements may produce an optimum morphological arrangement and an intricacy of functions that are able to spread beneficially into the surrounding city, beyond the borders of the planned area itself.

Great international events, exhibitions, celebrations, and productive economic upheavals have called for research into new design aptitudes that are capable of fulfilling the urgent need for innovation of the urban and territorial whole. Since the 1980s, the "special projects," which are measured against the building of Grand Paris (Greater Paris) and connected to the urban events related to the Barcelona Olympics, the Lisbon World Exposition, the decommissioning of the ports in Amsterdam and Hamburg, the rehabilitation of the London Dockland, and the reunification of Berlin (to name only a few events), attempt to recognize effective methods for managing ongoing and urgent processes of urban change. This transformation is not only concerned with the aspects of construction, as in postwar periods of reconstruction or the urban expansion of the 1960s. Now it collides with infrastructures, the historic city and urban sprawl, the landscape, the new conditions of urban spatial structure, new customs, and new lifestyles.

The restructuring of production, the returning of infrastructures and discarded systems into the heart of the city, demand practices to renew the existing city starting from the "brownfield" sites and no longer from the "greenfield" – the surrounding vacant land. The phenomenon of recentralization, the rediscovery of the advantages of the "compact city," as opposed to urban sprawl, requires a reconsideration of existing historical nuclei not only in conservationist or simplistic protectionist terms. The environmental crises demand reflections concerning sustainable growth and pose the question of developing the city upon itself without eating into land resources. The new range of investments, called for by the financial reorganization of public and private workers during a situation of economic crisis, leads to the development of sophisticated transformation programs. New relocations, new functions, and traditions materializing in the cities – different modes of enjoying the metropolitan landscape reflected in the weakening of the fundamentalist notion of "inhabiting the place" – force us to reformulate the large issues connected to the home, services, public space, and transportation, and to infrastructures of mobility.

Through the multiplicity of approaches, the city spaces illustrated in this book respond to such a set of problems, acting within the concrete reality of the transformations and synchronizing action and reflection. What shines through from this is the implementation of a set of variable practices and criteria that do not possess defining capabilities, but they do glow with the strength of tools forged for the occasion. The methods of urban renewal works, a fragmentary and temporary multiplicity of them, emerging from the *"mille plateaux"* (Deleuze and Guattari 1980) seem to follow cross-routes with respect to traditions, uncover unexpected connections, and provide limited answers with an awareness of acting in a transitory and variable state.

Parallel to the need to rethink city changes in their entirety, faith in the traditional planning tools has been lost because they are incapable of addressing urban development, contributing to a dynamics of development that make the city attractive, and creating a morphological and spatial quality. In the majority of cases, in fact, these special projects, in modifying large parts of the city, leave behind traditional regulative mechanisms because they are no longer able to respond to the changed requirements and actually become invalid because of partial variants or specific and sectoral alternative procedures: Zones d'Aménagement Concerté, Enterprise Zones, Local Plans, Piani d'area, Proyecto estratégico, public works projects, and others.

Certain key questions posed at the start of urban development activity must be considered at the time of planning: What is the relationship between plan and projects, between local plan and general plan, between a plan intended as a model to pursue or a plan intended as a process of management following shared principles and policies? New hopes, on the other hand, have been put on architecture, calling for the speculative and heuristic capacity of the project. Architecture competitions or international consultations, from which strategies have resulted that have led to the completion of those city sections illustrated here, have steered us towards the forming of a question, more than to a solution to problems not yet clearly identified. The architect has been asked to reveal, through the running of the project, what others would not have been able to see.

This additional question of performance is, in a certain sense, a natural part of the urban plan that occasionally perceives new shapes and relations between existing urban realities and tears apart morphological and programmatic conventions, taking on a "Popperian" function of clarification and correction of the hypotheses, projections, and indicated strategies. In this sense, the urban plan acquires strategic values and therefore operates on the level of real local transformation through a qualitative control of the city's morphology; but, at the same time, the urban plan participates in the launching of an overall renewal strategy, less and less expressed through traditional planning tools. Among its more meaningful results, availing itself of its ability to remove imperceptions and find themes in the activity and managing of the project itself, the urban plan, in fact, does not only take on a support role in the organization of operations: instead, it constitutes a determining factor in the formation of syntheses and the creation of opportunities.

In the choice of planner for Euralille, an urban quarter in Lille, France, for example, the necessary strategic value at play was very clear to the leadership of the management company. The person in charge, Rem Koolhaas, was chosen by international consultation. A "director" is capable of building an urban vision out of the questions raised - not a finished project or a morphological proposal but a way to implement the project. Even the plan for the Vila Olimpica del Poblenou, in tackling the problem of athlete housing, offers something different to the city: namely, the reacquisition of the beachfront and making kilometres of abandoned beaches usable. Out of the need to salvage discarded and marginalized areas, the Zones d'aménagement concerté (ZAC) de Bercy project in Paris reveals a strategy of designing a new park on a city scale, able to provide both symbolic and real "centrality" to the settlement and produce "urban added value."

The urban plan thus conceived calls for the delegation of management to one person so that he or she may direct the planning and execution phases, govern and regulate the different contributions, or justify the continuous adjustments. A director coordinates the work of others, defines each manufactured artifact and building in relation to distinct principles, guarantees results, and ensures that public opinion is satisfied and the clientele's needs fulfilled.

This approach, defined as a "coordinated urban project," is successful when the granting of responsibility takes place on the inside of a cultural unity and of a commonality of purpose between designer and client, both public and private, and in mutual recognition of and respect for different aims and intentions. Famous on this count are the partnerships, cemented by common civic commitment, between the mayor of Barcelona, Pasqual Maragall, and Oriol Bohigas, or between Lille's mayor and French prime minister Pierre Mauroy and Rem Koolhaas. More oriented towards the logic of entrepreneurial success is the bond between Leopoldo Pirelli and Vittorio Gregotti or between the management of Debis and Renzo Piano. In some countries, such as France, Germany, and the Netherlands, the coordinator architect as planner/director, is an established figure, and his or her contribution is expected in all urban projects that involve changes to large parts of the city and require the presence of multiple planners.

The start of a coordinated urban project implies the participation of various technical and planning, administrative, legal, and financial jurisdictions that, united in complex structures of public, private, or mixed management, perform the role of interface between client, designer, public administration, and the changing actors involved, governing the operation from the moment of setting up to completion. Public or mixed agencies, such as Nisa and Vosa, are purposely constituted to manage the implementation and completion of the Vila Olimpica, as well as Semest for Bercy, Semapa for Seine Rive Gauche, HafenCity Hamburg GmbH for HafenCity, or Saem for Euralille. Private multinational corporations, such as Pirelli or Daimler-Benz, have entrusted the management and real estate development of the areas in their possession to regulated agencies, designated for this purpose.

To launch a coordinated urban project, first and foremost, it is necessary to:
- facilitate the construction of a relatively unified and recognizable part of the city, and, at the same time, introduce those elements of differentiation and subdivision that can produce a morphological variety and richness of functions, which are appreciated in the allocated city;
- allow the city to be built over time, indicating at the moment of its conception the germinal features of its development, the "genetic code" of its growth;
- create opportune conditions to regulate the individual inputs (planners, workers, administrators, citizens) in a consensual play that may produce mutual enrichment – not a designer that imposes a solution, but shared hypotheses upon which to mediate the divergences, articulate requests, and satisfy aspirations;
- produce a compatible degree of flexibility to embrace opportunities and occasions along the way. It is becoming more and more difficult, if not impossible, to set up a definitive program and set firm goals. The planning of a vast section of a city must be able to incorporate resources and opportunities encountered during the implementation;
- guarantee high levels of sustainable development, in both environmental and social terms. A new part of a city must be efficient in terms of saving non-renewable resources. And at the same time, it must know how to be open to social plurality and the multiplicity of functions, without creating rifts with the existing city and its inhabitants;
- provide opportunities so that the sectoral and specialized planning (building, infrastructure, landscape) may find common ground and areas of agreement on goals.

The urban development plan triggers a cumulative and exponential "process": in the end, the value of the whole must be greater than the sum of the individual parts. Whereas, in the modern and contemporary city, often the equation is the reverse, and the value of the sum of the parts produces a negative balance: chaos, congestion, malfunction, decrease in environmental quality, and the degradation of spaces.

It is necessary, however, to be aware of the inappropriateness of relying upon the abstract virtue of the processes. The suitability of a process is confirmed only by the achieved results. Thus, only a few of the many urban projects launched in Europe, such as the ones presented in this volume, are providing satisfactory results in terms of quality. This demonstrates that the procedures are validated via ideational and planning content and, in the area of a discipline such as urban and architectural planning, the talent of the person exercising this profession is certainly not a secondary component. On the other hand, one cannot simply put one's trust entirely in individual talent. In the planning of cities, global demiurges so far have not revealed themselves capable of issuing effective and successful solutions upon request. Often, trusting in the presumed god-like abilities of a key player results in overlooking inadequacies in decision making regarding primary policies. It is also possible that these global demiurges themselves, caught in a vicious circle, become a function of demagogic operations and easily approved research.

The focus of the coordinated urban plan pertains to the quality of urban life, both physical and developmental, and to the implementation of good practices that will bring about quality results in the work of transforming and renovating the city itself. When themes tied to a city's "quality of life" are raised, often counterarguments that tend to minimize the issue come up: everyone, of course, maintains that "urban quality" is relevant but only after having dealt with the supposedly more important urgencies or problems. And the "more important problems" are considered to be those inherent in economic and social issues, environmental sustainability, or the future destiny of the city, as if all that could be tackled within a city without thinking of the physical and spatial model of the city itself and, therefore, the quality of city life as a whole.

We have by now seen the pernicious effects of an idea that tends toward the separation of elements seen as "structural" (economic, functional, infrastructural aspects) and those seen as "superstructural" or pertaining to aesthetics and quality, and therefore considered ephemeral. But the examples in this book show the courage of those who consider the quality of urban life fundamental and demonstrate the beneficial effects of a way of thinking that, in the transformation and renewal of cities, believes that a strong connection between economic revival, the building of infrastructure, and the qualitative transformation of the physical composition of the city must exist.

This connection is not about bestowing surpluses that have been produced, but must be recognized as a more complex and articulate strategy for overcoming the crises and dramatic phases of economic, social, and urban emergency, such as those that Europeans are currently experiencing.

In examining what has happened in these cities, what emerges as desirable is both the synergy between economic and qualitative issues in urban transformation and the ability to graft "projects" of physical transformation onto the "policies" of the city as a whole. By "policies" we mean those courageous acts of urban revival that some administrators, even when facing dramatic moments of urban, economic, and social crisis, have initiated and conducted during their electoral mandate and that, shared by large segments of citizens, are pursued for years, during different administrations, until their felicitous conclusion.

We refer here to the policies and processes of urban modernization, outlined in the slogan "Paris se lève à l'est" ("Paris rises in the east"), launched in the 1980s by Jacques Chirac, mayor of Paris, with the grandiose development plan aimed at revitalizing the whole of the east end of Paris, which had been considered an inferior area since the era of Georges-Eugène Haussmann (1853–70). We refer also to the policies of reviving the waterfront of Barcelona after the 1992 Olympics, initiated by Mayor Maragall with the famous phrase, "The Olympics last for fifteen days but the city lasts forever," and carried on by the International Forum of Culture in 2004. We also call attention to the strategies initiated in Amsterdam and Hamburg to revive the harbour docks, following on the heels of the dramatic economic crisis associated with the upheaval of the maritime transport systems and the traffic interchange.

We must learn from the parts of the city illustrated in this book. Their development constitutes a motive for a public and private sense of improvement. These initiatives make their citizens proud and interest urban scholars and tourists. They have enhanced what has been revealed as one of the most important assets of the city: the gift of a physical and spatial quality and its availability for the enjoyment of inhabitants and visitors.

*Compact City as Intensity City*
To better reflect on the methods of innovation for the existing city, it is necessary to return to the discussion of the negative consequences of urban sprawl that began in the 1990s, which leads us to the current theses mapped out in the domain of urban ecology around the models deemed sustainable in the building of the city.

The criticisms of urban sprawl involve various aspects. From the environmental point of view, urban sprawl would contribute to worsening global deterioration, with an increase in pollution and a waste of energy and land resources. The discrepancies in terms of suitability for human life and the problematical conditions of governance that collide with social reality are also still apparent. Negative economic implications are connected to the burdensome public investments and the high private costs that the inefficiencies of this development modality entail. The appeals in defence of the "compact city" as a "sustainable" urban form are taking up more and more space in the contemporary debate (Aa.Vv. 1996; Mostafavi and Doherty 2010).

The controversy around city models and the principles of development to adopt in the new urban spaces seems crucial, precisely in relation to the issues of environmental, social, and economic sustainability, and to those of the quality of life in contemporary residential areas as a whole. The dichotomy between "city sprawl" and "compact city," far from being an academic diatribe between architects, urban planners, sociologists, and ecologists, entails more general problems that require statements of positions in the larger decision-making and governing systems concerning economic, environmental, and welfare state strategies: the choices inherent in land infrastructure development and the policies of public transport, those of safeguarding the environment and land use, the control of energy consumption, and the defence of non-renewable resources.

It is interesting to examine a possibly deep disparity between different nations in the choice between the model of urban sprawl or of a compact city in reference, for example, to one of the more easily "measurable" parameters – specifically, residential density. In European cities, there is an oscillation in settlement density, which varies between twenty-five and one hundred residential units per hectare, considering that there are ten single-family dwellings with garden in one hectare. In Los Angeles, the average is fifteen houses; in the British new towns, as in the towns of northern Europe in the 1960s, the density is not higher than twenty-five dwellings. The average density in London is forty-two units, while in the historic centres of continental Europe, the average is around ninety units. The real estate developments of the 1970s in Singapore reached a density of 250 units. Even higher densities, up to 400 units per hectare, are present in some real estate developments of Beijing, Tokyo, and Seoul. But attempts to enact higher densities are also being made in the Netherlands, in the waterfront reclamation zones, and in certain limited areas in Amsterdam, Paris, and London that are especially responsive to and rich in collective mobility infrastructure development.

Numerous studies have shown that an out-of-town bus service is sustainable, in terms of costs and benefits, for twenty-five units or more per hectare. A tram service is adequate for a density of sixty units. In some urban sections, which function as interchanges of collective and private urban and suburban transit largely because of highly developed infrastructure, it is desirable to encourage hubs of centrality with a higher density of settlement so as to enjoy the advantages of privileged accessibility permitted by collective transport and the synchronous presence of practices that would reduce displacements.

Resorting to high density and the compact city is, therefore, not to be understood as a nostalgic and ideological return to the "city as a work of art," nor solely as an openness to opportunities of economic forces and real estate investment. The compact city is better understood as a condition of sustainable development.

But the compact city is also a critical sphere of operation that continuously demands the testing of the values of contemporary architectural and urban planning: the blending of settlement configurations, the updating of building types, the reformulation of infrastructures, the occasional building of models of social cohabitation. The compact city, understood as a city of high physical, social, and relational density, a synergistic melting pot of more customs, functions, and rituals, is also a privileged domain for smart policies aimed at living, working, and leisure. The compact city model allows for the reduction of physical displacements from home to work and home to play and recreational activities, which diminishes social and environmental costs of private and public transport. It allows us to optimize the impact of land and urbanization investment costs. It creates the conditions for synergy between the existing city and these newly built urban areas and facilitates the processes of social integration in the mixing of housing structures and centres for social interaction.

Furthermore, within the compact city model, it is possible to promote urban renewal processes on existing property by advocating building replacement, to trigger processes of recuperation of marginalized areas, and to support policies of total regeneration of entire areas of the city in decline. Thus, a resurgence of lifestyles, related to the social and working conditions that are undergoing change, is also facilitated.

However, beyond the ecological, environmental, and economic issues, one also has to evaluate aspects pertaining to quality of life because, as Michael Sorkin maintains (2003), "it is important to distinguish between density and extension. After all there is density and there is density: we have to distinguish between the quality of Jones Beach on a sun-lit afternoon or the hustle and bustle of Fifth Avenue in the week before Christmas from the crowdedness of the Warsaw Ghetto or from the suffocating black hole of Calcutta. Density can produce efficiency and pleasure, or create a nightmare." Sorkin attempts to define density phenomenologically, since it is capable of generating an increase in the quality of life in cities, and he highlights different types. Physical density would bring us back to the spatial character of the traditional city. On the other hand, social and environmental density, expressed in terms of relationships, customs, and interactions, would allow the benefits offered by the specific idiosyncrasies of the metropolis to filter through. If, as he says, "the political and social life of the metropolis does not simply depend on the encounter itself but on its structure[,] a good city is a vehicle that produces happy accidents, not a mechanism that generates collisions" (Sorkin 2003).

A metropolis is more than a scenario for the celebration of continuous flux and inexplicable dynamism, as in some visions of contemporary "neo-futurism." It is also the place of the casual encounter, of the episodic interaction, the playing field of an encounter or a clash between the different social roles and spheres, the stage of that "theatrical performance" to which Erwin Goffman (1997) attributes social life and the multilayered and always temporary structure of every single image.

The anthropologist Ulf Hannerz (1992) had already invited us in his book *Exploring the City: Inquiries towards an Urban Anthropology* "to see the city as a place where we can find one thing while looking for another." This definition makes us glimpse the possibility of "living" in the known part of the city, but also "to wander" elsewhere, as suggested by Walter Benjamin (2007), and encounter the unexpected. This trait, unique to a large city or metropolis, entails a dangerous fascination and stimulated a blasé attitude in inhabitants of the emerging metropolis in the early twentieth century – something that troubled Georg Simmel so much but at the same time attracted him. It is an element of potential openness in the creation of new identities, freed from the rigid physical and social determinism of historical places. The large city and the metropolis thus clearly distinguished themselves from the village, town, or small city where, according to Max Weber's classic definition and according to the illusions of the "cultural planning" founded by John Ruskin and William Morris, a connection between physical reality and community would persist.

"Finding one thing while looking for another," known as serendipity, involves the use of a structure created for functions different from those that have governed the structure's existence. Massimo Piattelli Palmarini (1985) clarifies the process by using the example of a sensational case of serendipitous use within the field of scientific research: Palmarini, during his experiments, found that the wings of insects evolved primarily to exchange warmth with the surrounding environment, but, flying, the secondary evolution function, has revealed itself the more important function. A felicitous attempt of marrying the concept of serendipity with the urban experience was proposed by Arnaldo Bagnasco (1994) and was thus formulated: "the variety of experiences that the city allows, the multiplicity of different situations in which one is involved allows city dwellers new and unexpected cultural syntheses … Secondly, the city is large enough, it contains a sufficiently large number of people to make it so that the casual intermingler is able to meet someone else capable of finding similarities, and willing to cultivate with him/her the possibilities of a new connection."

Variety and an increase in the possibilities of interaction, coupled with a relative "uncertainty" and a sufficient "wealth" and "density" of meaning and of valuable offers, are therefore necessary conditions so that serendipity may occur. Mono-functional cities, neighbourhoods that produce social uniformity, collective spaces, specializing in the uniformity of consumers — ultimately the Fordist city, constructed around functional and homogeneous zones, and the sprawl that produces only those hyper-specialized ones of shopping centres and intermodal transport hubs as collective spaces — generate instead low levels of serendipity.

From the reaction to the low density of urban sprawl, two theoretical and working tendencies seem to emerge. One, defined as new urbanism, is oriented towards the recovery of the spatial nature of the traditional city, of the city "on a human scale," in which the proportions on the micro-social scale hoped for by Jane Jacobs (1961) that once again fascinate the followers of urban ecology would find fulfillment. The other, defined as post-urbanism would be induced instead to celebrate the advantages of metropolitan "congestion," all flux and dynamic energy, as it appears in some writings on "Manhattism" and the "Bigness" of Rem Koolhaas (1978; 1995).

Thus, we have two antithetical visions: the "pastoral" and the "explosive," to draw on Marshall Berman (1991), but both bring back again the discussion about an "alternative" to the existing city. Between a veiled irritation with urban life underlying the "pastoral" image and the "explosive" image of the propulsive forces of the new dynamics,

it is necessary to rediscover the terms of a new transitional situation: an "intensity city," which, without the nostalgic reproposing of the city of the past, achieves a combination of issues and subjects emerging within the metropolitan scale — intensity of changes, exchanges, and experiences — in the existing city, according to a "pact," an agreement between inherited form and new urban contents.

The inexorable progressive interpenetration of urban zones into the landscape and vice versa, of environmental and landscape themes in the restructuring of urban sprawl, or in the building, development of infrastructure, and improvement of the existing city, seems in fact to support the formation of the intensity city. We can verify this in the examples provided in this book. Infrastructure planning becomes involved with landscape topics; in turn, landscape design, with renewed energy, returns to play a strategic, dense, and meaningful role in the city; urban design, embracing the metropolitan horizon, sees the new infrastructure and landscape configurations as opportunities and possibilities to free itself from the models of the past.

In the contemporary metropolitan situation, we are seeing methods of urban construction that invert the past three decades' methods. On the one hand, sprawl emerges as a new reality to retrieve and bring us back to the requisite suitability for human habitation. On the other hand, the depletion of usable areas within the city leads to a search for ways and means to achieve new urban expansions. In the transition from the construction of the "city within the city" to the restoration of urbanized land, the emerging forms of settlement, as they blend with the new models of infrastructure landscapes, seem to possess the art and technique to tackle unexpected design challenges.

Classifying new usages, including different forms and gradients of density, and interweaving historic reality with the new dynamic reality, incorporating landscape and environmental facts, integrating what is known with the innovative, inevitably brings problems and criticisms. Different approaches to urban planning, as they appear in this book, have been revealed as possible remedies and suitable measures for guiding the terms of this transitional situation. In trying to legitimize the demands for change in the framework of a newly discovered urban culture, these approaches to urban planning participate in the dynamics of the current unstable metropolitan situation and of the values of the existing city. These approaches to urban planning represent a multiform problematic and complex practice, which incorporates plans for open spaces, infrastructures, and buildings on a wider horizon: accommodating and simultaneously transcending the open spaces, infrastructures, and the buildings themselves. They constitute a higher responsibility to design that creates greater realities. Each project becomes a time for giving shape to both city and landscape in a process of mutual exploration and "in a perpetual movement of systoles and diastoles with the surroundings," as Ignasi de Solà-Morales so insightfully writes (2001). A strong civic commitment shines through in this present inclination to organize, preserve, articulate, and integrate the new with the existing and the old with modernization.

# **Almere**, Stadshart

On the edges of the Randstad, the city of Almere extends over a territory of 120 km$^2$, snatched from the sea by vast works of reclamation. In 1972, sociologists, ecologists, architects, economists, and landscape architects, organized into an interdisciplinary group, began to plan the new city by examining the new town of Milton Keynes north of London and the residential suburbs at the doors of the great American cities. Building a city for three hundred thousand inhabitants in a few years is surely a complex enterprise, rather risky and with uncontrollable final results. Consequently and conveniently, a morphological structure is placed at the cornerstone of the operation as a polynuclear system of growth over time, clearly revealing the skepticism in the ability of the forecast procedures to program and globally control a decades-long urban development.

As it took shape, the unfolding of the project strategically wove together a comprehensive planning model with the empiricism of incremental adjustments. Arranged like an amphitheatre, around the lake basin of the Weerwater and along the connecting highway and railway lines to the other cities of the Randstad, three nuclei were built in different times and according to different methods: Almere-Haven to the south, Almere-Stad in the centre, and Almere-Buiten to the northwest.

Now Almere, the largest garden city of Europe, is a sprawl of single-family dwellings. By 2020 the population will grow to four hundred thousand inhabitants, entering the circle of the five largest cities of the Netherlands. But the settlement reality remains dispersed, so scattered within the landscape as to be difficult to discern in its physical and spatial consistency. Since the 1990s, the municipality, with a succession of expansion and densification projects, has tried to give it an urban character.

Satisfying the demand for new spaces devoted to culture, leisure time, and work, OMA-Rem Koolhaas won an international competition forum in 1994 to give the form and identity of "centre" to Almere-Stad. With rather expressive urban models, two focal points of attraction were configured. While one piece of metropolitan complexity, an exercise in urban syntax, is evoked by the piling up of buildings built near the Zakencentrum railroad station, the second model, around the theme of urban structure and layout, appears at the Stadscentrum, facing onto the lake basin of the Weerwater and destined to be a residential space with recreational and cultural activities.

OMA focuses the settlement in only two areas in order to create an urban identity with an elevated density and a strong intrinsic image – the hoped-for "quantum leap." Practically speaking, Koolhaas's plan responds to two different exigencies at the same time: a provision for offices and directional spaces, something that a real estate market, at the scale of the entire Randstad, requires for expanded railroad accessibility; and the localization, within the fabric of the city, of urban fixtures, accessible by car, and functional for the entire residential suburb. It superimposes two density models and, at the same time, two different ways of living the urban experience. The overcrowded metropolis interweaves infrastructures, workplaces, and centres for interaction according to the "Manhattanism" so dear to Koolhaas, but also placed here with more scrupulousness when compared to Euralille. The low-rise compact city binds the rituals of pedestrianism and strolling with contemporary consumer models, like shopping and entertainment. Koolhaas offers the fascination of "otherworldliness" to the lifestyles and spatiality of a garden city: he tries, as much as possible and in a short time, to substitute a ready-made urban identity, complete with an operational process of real estate development.

Where, in a vicious cycle, multiplexes, casinos, shopping centres, exhibition and recreation centres, parking lots, and business centres usually feed the contemporary urban sprawl, here, instead, the opposite settlement principles apply: they call for building an "intensity" city in parts, and in others, for instilling urban traditions.

The centre, a kind of pedestrian top plate resting on twenty-five hectares of parking space, is new ground to subdivide into city blocks that imitate an urban fabric. It is a collage of discontinuous and subtle elements that recalls Kahn or Ungers in some projects of the 1970s. The waterfront, dedicated to cultural and leisure activities, is organized around a spectacular sequence of landscaped loops and landmarks.

Welcoming the futuristic visions of the mechanized metropolis, the traffic arteries, residential units, and accesses to buildings and roads, emphasized by the superimposing and the interweaving of the flow of communication, radiate outward, with the vitality of a pulsating circulating organism. The parking area, a large covered "dock," is illuminated by the reverberations of the shore, which it overlooks. The individual parking bays, marked by painted backgrounds of different colours with different degrees of sheen, allude to the perceptual values of the water's refraction and visibly extend the effects of the light of the lake basin right into the parking area. It is onto this privileged spot, which is finally risen to the collective role, in a dynamic network of information, accesses, arrivals, and departures – where every activity – converges. And it is here that lobbies of the buildings open. The pulsating current of the physical and perceptual movements reaches and mixes with the city above.

Prophesied by Hénard in the Rue Future, the elevated city encountered the enthusiasm of Le Corbusier in the Ville Radieuse and Hilberseimer in the Idealstadt Entwurf. In the past, the benefits and merits of such a system of complexes, layered in sections, had already been widely proclaimed with respect to the traditional city rooted to the ground. Only after the Second World War was the elevated city able to find practical application, re-initiated out of the heroism of the Archigram and Metabolist projects and those of some exponents of Team X, even if this application was in close association with those principles of CIAM that preached division between transport and utilization, between vehicular traffic and human circulation. The Défense in Paris, the Part Dieu in Lyon, the Barbican in London – to cite the most well-known examples – are developments, on different scales and levels of complexities of usage, of the elevated city, in the permutation of the model predicated on functionalist precepts, indissolubly tied to the principle of separation.

What would differentiate the new centre of Almere from these projects of the 1960s, for many, a fulfillment of the presentiment of the death of the city? The sectionalized complex, common to both, here in Almere does not involve any principle of separation: not in the flows of traffic from the movements of people, nor of ease of access from activities. There is no separation between the buildings and the open spaces, between the collective sphere and the private sphere. In Almere, separation is driven out by the hybridization and co-existence of customs, structures, and experiences. Different areas are also mixed on the "top plate" so that they may interact in a more complete and user-friendly process.

Koolhaas substitutes a continuity of a cinematic nature for a phenomenology of fragmentary perceptions, and makes it so that the cinematic narrative might involve even the spheres of transition and exchange between the different practices – no longer marginalized fringes but "thresholds" that register, in the reality of things, what Benjamin calls "tectonic and ceremonial" rites. With material belonging to contemporary architecture, with structures, suitable but new, and with pertinent subjects, Koolhaas demonstrates that he knows how to physically and symbolically represent new rites of passage, and succeeds in transforming the parking space into the largest public space in the city.

When analyzing what has been built up till now, a gap seems to place itself between intentions and results, however.

The collage-like approach to the "block" of OMA is surely compatible with the partitions between designers, and is practical for the site set-up in distinct phases. The design coordination, moreover, would seem to help market aspirations, allowing the different "brands," glorified by design "labels," to stand out like symbols in competition, similar to Venturian Las Vegas.

The residential buildings along the lake by Claus en Kaan and F. van Dongen, the entertainment and reception centre of Alsop, the multiplex of OMA, the residential and commercial complex of D. Chipperfield, the "theme park" by C. de Portzamparc for residential and commercial use, beyond their individual architectural qualities, seem, in their totality, to have achieved a pure juxtaposition of heterogeneous building complexes. On the other hand, the specific plan of each block, developed separately and autonomously, without links of reciprocity, seems to emerge in fits and spasms. The organization into thematically discontinuous blocks today would seem to be reduced to different "allegorical worlds" to be accessed one after the other through various routes and open spaces – momentary approaches, distinct "cinematic sets."

It also seems that the mix of proposed functions and the variety of projects reflects a feverish pursuit of the opportunities of the real estate and consumer market, excessively pandering to contingencies and mainly trusting in the spectacle factor. The centre of Almere, like a great exhibition, a gigantic commercial mall in the open, or a theme park, thus runs the risk of being chained to the short-lived cycle of events and consumption habits, risking a speedy obsolescence.

The Stadttheater, Almere's monument to art and culture for which Saana won the international competition in 1999, seems to resist these impulses. It is a slim and transparent platform positioned on the water and subdivided into exhibition spaces, ateliers, and gardens by glass-panelled diaphragms and moving walls. The theatre spaces rise up, like silent icons, from this glassed-in raft, projected between water and sky. They distinguish themselves as essential and to the point amid the exuberant spectacles of the surrounding buildings.

**Almere**, Stadshart

Urban plan and coordination: OMA
Development company: Stadshart Almere – MAB Development
Planning and implementation: 1994–2012

 1 Theatre: SANAA
 2 Side by Side: F. van Dongen
 3 Silverline: Claus en Kaan
 4 The Whale: R. van Zuuk
 5 Bridge: R. van Zuuk
 6 Swamp Garden: Inside/Outside
 7 Hotel: Alsop Architects
 8 Casla: Lanoire & Courrian
 9 Esplanade: M. Desvigne
10 Utopolis: OMA
11 The City: van Sambeek
12 De Citadel: C. de Portzamparc
13 The Jewel: D. Chipperfield
14 Bibliotheek Almere: Meyer & van Schooten
15 Smaragd: Gigon & Guyer
16 Commerce: De Architectengroep
17 Angle: S333
18 Railroad station
19 World Trade Center: De Architekten Cie
20 La Défense: UNStudio

# Amsterdam, Borneo Sporenburg, Oostelijk Havengebied

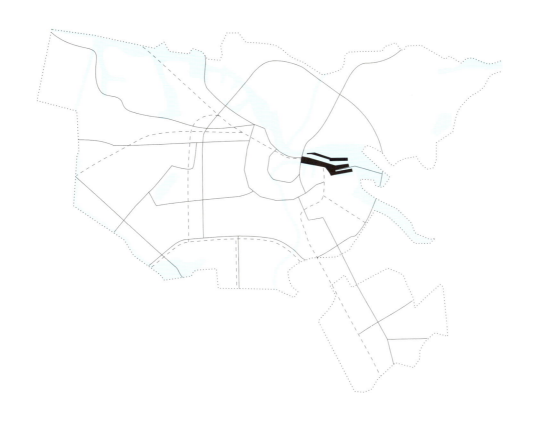

The current structural layout of Amsterdam's Oostelijk Havengebied is an obvious consequence of a change of course in contemporary Dutch urban design. The push in the 1970s to coordinate urban planning and public housing construction became weaker and weaker, following the economic crisis that forced an acceleration of welfare state reform. Public housing construction became privatized, ending the long marriage of planning and residential programming that had distinguished Dutch urban policies since the time of the Woningwet, a 1901 law on residential buildings.

In the 1980s, in addition to the economic crisis public housing planning and construction, urban density as an alternative to sprawl became a significant issue. In the great port cities, the necessity of revitalizing the areas of the nineteenth-century docks, which are mostly situated in strategic areas of the urban structure, also became an important issue.

In Amsterdam, in particular, the transformation of the docks, extending through the entire Oostelijk Haven and onto the artificial peninsulas of KNSM, Java, Borneo, and Sporenburg, became not only an occasion of urban development but also an occasion to generally rethink the city, which involved road, railroad, and public transportation reform.

Beginning in 1987, the strategic plan for the area of Oostelijk Haven, formulated by the Dienst Ruimtelijke Ordening (DRO), the department of urban planning of the municipality, leaves intact the port basins, and arranges for high building density, according to the morphological principles of Rem Koolhaas's master plan of 1983. Exiting between Borneo and Sporenburg, the road and tramway linkage tunnel connects the city with the territorial road network of the peninsulas, thus promoting the redevelopment of the areas. The housing program, mainly residential, with almost ten thousand dwellings and their relative services, was subdivided into three urban projects, entrusted, by means of consultation, to three planners outside the public administration. Between 1989 and 1993, Jo Coenen for KNSM, Sjoerd Soeters for Java, and West 8 for Borneo Sporenburg elaborated their respective master plans and superintended, as coordinators, the building designs entrusted to other architects. Following the directives of the master plan of 1997 by Hans van der Made of DRO, with the restructuring of the Handelskade, the railway yard, the areas east of the train station were also involved in the urban dynamic. The docks could finally become connected, physically and gratifyingly, with the city centre. And a new urban continuity now extends for more than four kilometres.

In this grandiose scheme of urban renewal and development, the public is reserved the fundamental tasks of promoting, planning, and verifying the economic and qualitative results, besides negotiating with the private investors, to whom the building rights are transferred, and selecting the planners and a percentage of the public sector buildings, not different, in terms of quality and standards, from the ones destined for the market.

Echoing the Dutch public housing development of the 1970s, partially updated with the renewal of urban agreements, J. Coenen assembles a sequence of residential superblocks along the central axis of the KNSM: the Piraeus of H. Koolhoff, the Emerald Empire of the same J. Coenen, the Langhaus of Diener & Diener. These urban landmarks – the so-called "Urban Giant" – stand out on the scale of the harbour landscape, even though they still express an established housing dimension.

In Java, a sequence of five super city blocks, circumscribed by street-canals, is based on the experience of the *hofe* of Amsterdam South and blends models of urban density with an opening in the landscape: an internal garden crosses the development lengthwise to accommodate schools and neighbourhood services. To evoke the complex layering of the historic city, a principle of cadastral subdivision is simulated here in a combination game in which different architects participate, including Cruz & Ortiz, S. Soeters, Kerelse & van der Meer, and Geurst & Schulze. To create an empirical urban culture, one draws on the experiments of "architectural polyphony" by R. Krier to Iba 84, reinterpreted by O. Bohigas in the Vila Olimpica, the random "surrealist montage" by A. Rossi to the Friedrichstrasse, or the typological collages of O.M. Ungers to the Lutzoplaz of Berlin. Even if, due to excessive fragmentation, the result of employing this "architectural polyphony" may not succeed on the large scale of the harbour spaces, it truly works on the small scale of the street. The waterfront along the Handelskade, however, certainly bears the stamp of the large scale, reclaiming the full scan of the old warehouses. The fusion of linear buildings along the piers, with high blocks along the infrastructure clusters, generates segments of metropolitan hyperdensity.

If, on the peninsulas of KNSM and Java, the real estate market is mostly built on lots and city blocks, in the neighbourhoods of Borneo Sporenburg, it has pushed for a suburban residential typology: single dwellings with separate facades and entrances opening onto the street. The municipality supported the demands of the investors, but at the same time imposed, as a non-negotiable parameter, an extremely high density of one hundred houses per hectare. The paradoxical convergence of suburban typologies and a dense city stimulated the invention of new housing typologies. West 8, winner in 1993 of the consultation called for by the New Deal, the development agency of the area, is grafting high-density onto low-rise, as opposed to other projects where, borrowing from the experience of New Urbanism, the *garden* suburb was again proposed.

The new structural layout takes advantage of the presence of the water and the port infrastructure, celebrating their landscape values. Used as materials, wind, air, light, perfumes, solar reflections, and refractions of the natural elements substantiate the project in the expression and optimization of this unusual urban setting. Houses overlooking the water are envisaged to enjoy the fortunate environmental features and offer housing quality, despite the scarcity of urban land.

Low buildings, organized in rigorous sections subdivided into plots, are structured in groups, similar to the colour field of the land, set aside for cultivation, rather than the organization of an urban fabric, and create a development built on the balance between continuity and variety. Alternating buildings with small clearings and enclosures with vast horizons distinguishes, in favourable interaction, the protected urban space from the opening onto wide vistas.

The regular weaving of these plots is interrupted by three sculptural building blocks known as the Meteorites, which appear to defy geometric principles. These buildings, exceptional in form and typology, contrast with the continuity of the parterre of the building fabric on three floors and respond to the demands of the large size of the city and river. The sculptural plasticity of these blocks of spaces, misshapen and worn down in order to open up extensive views and to be able to incorporate environmental values, like what sixteenth-century Flemish painting did with landscape, makes them stand out like recognizable signs of the expanse of the urban skyline, connects the sea of houses to the city and the landscape, and offers the opportunity to manipulate and renew the residential typologies.

To consider the urban fabric as a "metaphor" and not as a "model" allows us to act with open-mindedness, disturbs imagined certainties around the urban categories, and puts into context the opposing spheres of public and private. Avenues, allotments of land, and monuments – all emptied of every foundational value – are reduced to principles of morphological organization and the criteria of management and coordination (after all, thirty-five groups of architects were involved in the project) with relatively coherent results. The "secularization" of the city allows for the shift from acquired references – the Gothic allotment, the foundations, the canals – to individual elements, as well as the launch of a research project, that upset the categories of the city of the past. And thus, this "type," fruit of the multiple experiments around the plurality of housing models, will no longer entail repetition but variety, and the land "allotment," instead of guarding the private, will open, in terms of visuals and transparencies, onto the streets, the canals, and, as lofts and stores, will become a new form of "public" space.

The street, just a line and the beginning of a configuration, is denied as a public reality. The reduction of the conventional elements of the urban space coincides with the conferring of a collective value onto the seascape and the harbour basin – here a true "public place." Used in an instrumental sense, the relationship of "fabric" and "monument," the cornerstone of the urban concept, becomes a scenic pretext for opening onto vistas and transparencies in order to leave the city and communicate with the infrastructures of the harbour and the geographical totality.

A project of urban transformation that functions on a "midway scale," between building and city, cannot transcend the miniature scale of the individual building. Indeed, right from the start of the modernization of the building, it is possible to overthrow, in effect, the chains and conflicts of the morphological urban-scale concept. In the workshops that have started up, a clearinghouse between individuality and general strategy, besides being the sound box of creativity, offered the possibility of reinventing and enriching the principles of the project. Here, outside the shackles of academia or cultural association, architectural and typological research, oriented along morphological guidelines, united young architects with successful firms such as OMA, Mateo, De Architeckten Cie, Mvrdv, Holl, and Miralles. In a joint competition, they envisaged unconventional residential models: five base typologies and a rich spectrum of variables and distribution patterns. Without falling into abstract linguistic exercises or a compilation of virtuoso-like samples of personal styles, they were able to make the architectural and typological differentiation, developed along the way, functional to the configuration of a unity of wholes: a sea of houses, a continuity intended to produce an identity strong enough to evoke a landscape and geographical reality.

A minor network of routes is superimposed onto the regularity of the site and connects the two peninsulas by means of two bridges, designed by West 8, for their sculptural quality, a distinctive trait of the site. One runs along the water's edge; the other soars above, evoking the skeletal structure of a gigantic cetacean, and at the summit of its twenty metres in height, it becomes a lookout, opening onto the landscape of the roofs and the horizons of the port. A surplus of images and forms imparts energy to the neighbourhood and transforms the crossings into a playful and spectacular reality.

**Amsterdam**, Borneo Sporenburg, Oostelijk Havengebied

*Borneo Sporenburg*
Urban plan and coordination: West 8
Development company: New Deal
Planning and implementation: 1993–2000

*Java*
Urban plan and coordination: Sjoerd Soeters
Development company: Amsterdam Local Authority
Planning and implementation: 1994–2008

*KNSM*
Urban plan and coordination: Jo Coenen
Development company: Amsterdam Local Authority
Planning and implementation: 1987–1996

*Handelskade*
Urban plan and coordination: Dienst Ruimtelijke Ordening (DRO)
Development company: Amsterdam Local Authority
Planning and implementation: 1997–2013

1 The Bruggen: T. Venhoeven, J. Schaeferbrug
2 Residence: Cruz & Ortiz
3 Residence: K. Christiaanse
4 Residence: S. Soeters
5 Residence: Karelse & van der Meer
6 Hybrid building: Koetter & Salman
7 AWG: B. van Reeth
8 Hybrid building: CASA Architekten
9 Langhaus: Diener & Diener
10 Piraeus: H. Kollhoff
11 Skydome: W. Arets
12 Residence: B. Albert
13 Emerald Empire: J. Coenen
14 City block: N. Riedijk, Claus en Kaan, Köther en Salman, R. Visser
15 City block: Atelier Zeinstra, van Sambeek & van Veen
16 City block: Heren 5, van Sambeek & van Veen
17 City block: JHK
18 City block: DKV, Höhne & Rapp, van Sambeek & van Veen
19 City block: Claus en Kaan, Heren 5, M3H, van Sambeek & van Veen
20 The Whale: De Architekten Cie
21 City block: Atelier Zeinstra
22 City block: JHK
23 City block: Atelier Zeinstra, DKV, van der Donk, Höhne & Rapp
24 City block: Claus en Kaan, van Sambeek & van Veen
25 City block: Köther en Salman, van Sambeek & van Veen
26 City block: Claus en Kaan
27 City block: Claus en Kaan, JHK
28 House: UNStudio
29 House: E. Milralles
30 City block: Atelier Zeinstra, Tupker & van der Neut, S. Sorgdrager, van der Pol
31 De Pacman: K. Van Velsen
32 City block: K. Christiaanse
33 City block: De Architectengroep
34 City block: Faro Architecten, Marge Architecten, R. Uytenhaak
35 City block: R. Uytenhaak, Heren 5
36 City block: Tupker & van der Neut, Atelier Zeinstra, S. Sorgdrager
37 City block: L. Mateo, Van Herk en De Kleijn
38 Pedestrian bridges: West 8

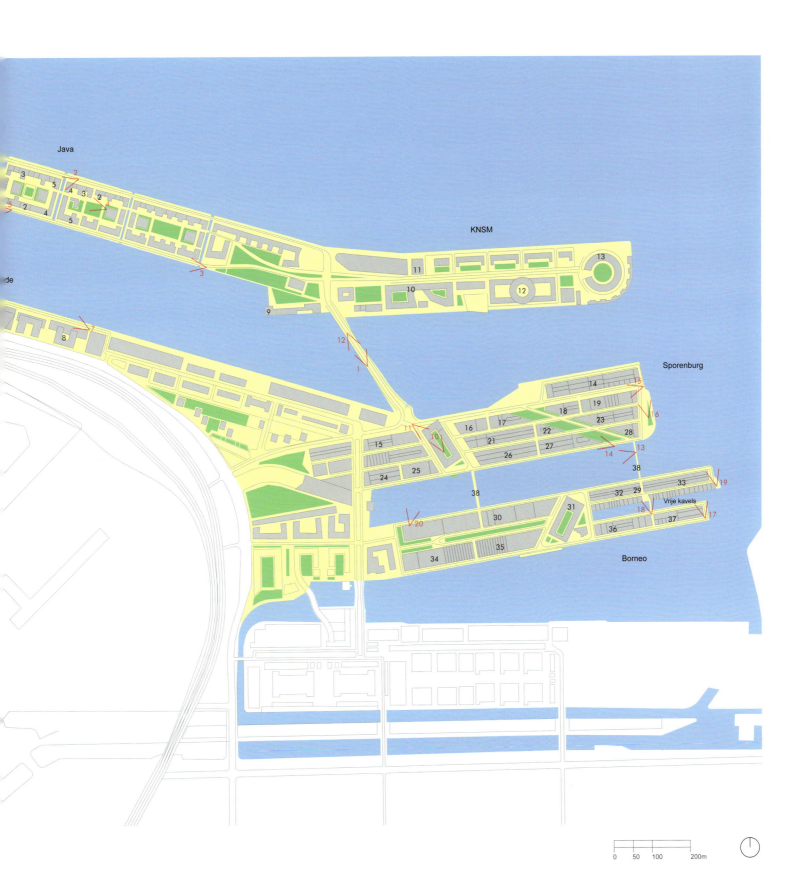

# Amsterdam, Zuidas

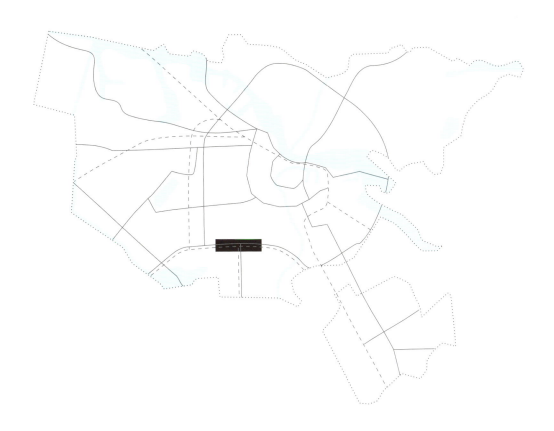

Zuidas, a section of the Southern Axis – the expansion plane along the highways between Amsterdam South and Schiphol airport – marks the turning point in the building processes of the Netherlands' cities and anticipates the developments in city building in Europe. During the 1980s, in the restoration of the existing city, density and infrastructure development was the core of the urban renewal program. Production upheavals and infrastructure reforms demanded a reorganization of disused (brownfield) sites and the waterfront.

A different set of circumstances greets the Zuidas project. The radical change in urban policies, initiated by neoliberal orientations, puts pressure on the urban design metamorphosis, raises fundamental questions, and leaves its mark on future developments. Overturning the previous tendency towards centralization, new expansions and forms of centrality outside the city are anticipated. The emphasis is placed on the economic optimization of the urban construction operations, satisfying the expectations of the current forms of real estate financialization. The infrastructures, interpreted in neo-Keynesian optics, call for a driving force in the relaunch of investments: if the issue of urban reform first occurred in association with the infrastructure reorganization, now it is the positional revenues, offered by a new topography of accessibility following the infrastructure developments in completion phase, that generate new development opportunities.

In evaluating the broad socioeconomic, environmental, and settlement implications, Zuidas cannot be considered as an incidental and transitory urban development created out of a chance convergence of factors, such as the closeness to the airport and the presence of operational areas and of infrastructures for urban mobility. Zuidas should be read as an experiment in the creation of a new urban centrality that does not originate from the existing city, as it still does for Euralille, Seine Rive Gauche, and Potsdamer Platz. It represents the network's core of "global centralities," which in the space-time compression generated by a continental-scale system of communication, benefit from high levels of accessibility and, like the airports and high-velocity train stations, simultaneously enjoy the advantages and suffer the disadvantages of an atopic predisposition.

With the brownfield sites in the heart of the city recovered, with the rail yards being reused, and the renewal of the waterfront and docks, new settlement opportunities have opened up in conjunction with the infrastructure reforms of interchange mobility with the airports. The next development zone between Bilbao and Sondica Airport, the area of Porta Sud between the old city of Bergamo and the Milan Orio al Serio Airport, and the business parks that are developing around the airports of Luton and Heathrow in London and near the Frankfurt Airport show a compelling inclination to become global network hubs that transcend an urban and local dimension. Generated by the high level of intermodal and airport accessibility, enormous economic and social opportunities are begging to be managed. But it is necessary to break the habit of configuring mono-functional enclaves and instead direct resources towards the completion of truly multifunctional and vital segments of the city – "global centres," to quote Hall, Sassen, and Castells, that can moreover become hinges between a network of transnational connections and exchanges, and represent an opportunity for a shared rebirth and enrichment.

Zuidas satisfies these aspirations and represents an emblematic model. Engendering synergies, it interweaves three key aspects: the management of the stimulated economic potential, the configuring of a new framework of syntheses between urban and territorial policies, and the integration of numerous settlement aims.

The economic potential is the result of a convergence of interests: financial and real estate for the big Dutch banks that have been inclined to decentralize, concentrating their branches near the airport; and strategic for the municipality of Amsterdam, for whom it was urgent to reorganize the infrastructure allotments along the A10 and the lines of the high velocity trains. The agreement signed in 2000 by the managing organizations and the banks reaffirmed the private capital commitment to acquire the volumetric rights generated by the burying of the road and railroad lines from the public, in compensation for the public costs to renew the infrastructures.

But in the sphere of settlement policies, it also becomes necessary to alter the regulatory and procedural frame of reference. Zuidas makes pressing a regulative and legislative renovation and a renewal of the decision-making procedures comparable in importance to the abandoning of comprehensive planning, implemented by the "special projects" in the 1980s. In fact, it is necessary to find agreement between the decisions on the "local" level, which concern, for example, the placement of the new developments (mostly the jurisdiction of local agencies), and the decisions on the "general" level, which concern, for example, the programming and implementation of territorial infrastructures under the jurisdiction of the central government or sectoral agencies. Shattering rigidity and the separation of jurisdictions has allowed for the discovery of plans of convergence and the synergistic interweaving of infrastructure and city, two realities that are still difficult to merge today.

Creating a real and vital part of a city presupposes a high level of complexity and urban intensity. This means integrating multiple settlement aims and connecting different landscape and infrastructure, and ecological and environmentally sustainable perspectives in a profitable form of interaction. Zuidas embraces a complexity and multiplicity of functions; together with the residential neighbourhoods to the north and south that are now separated by infrastructure clusters, Zuidas involves neighbouring urban systems, the World Trade Centre, the headquarters of the Free University, and the RAI Exhibition Centre. Zuidas is a liveable city of offices but also of houses and gardens and pedestrian traffic and interchanges, which makes it different from the business district of the Défense or Canary Wharf, which were planned with an emphasis on work. In this case, the special reference goes to Seine Rive Gauche and Potsdamer Platz (as opposed to the Défense or Canary Wharf), where multifunctionality and the mixture of urban models really produce an urban character.

Already in the first master plan, drafted in 1998 by Pl de Bruijn, a partner in De Architekten Cie, in collaboration with the Dienst Ruimtelijke Ordening (DRO), the municipality's urban planning department, these directives were clearly unveiled. A new foundation of city blocks and urban lots extending between the shores of the infrastructure trench is intended to relate open spaces, parks, and gardens to the already established activities and the urban neighbourhood of Berlage to the north and the residential expansion of Van Eesteren to the south – an interpretation of the grid that leaves ample margins of flexibility in the configuration of buildings and spaces. A strategy of flexible development is implemented, one that is subject to adjustments and able along the way to embrace opportunities and absorb decision-making deadlocks. It represents an elasticity that shows itself to be beneficial in the wait for the discovery of a solution to the controversy, manifested in the alternative of dock or dike.

The issue of the infrastructure transit systems (highway, railroad, and underground) that, running in the centre of Zuidas, represents a development engine, in fact, reveals a critical difficulty in the choice of settlement model.

The solution of the dock, even though costly, would channel entirely through tunnels – the transit infrastructures that cut the development area in two – for over a kilometre. A large artificial deck covering the railroad yards, which has already been tried in New York, London, and Paris, would make possible the re-use of the added surfaces, allowing the new city to grow on top of streets and tracks. The increase of the land surface would add to the advantages offered by the reunification of the area and by the decrease in atmospheric and noise pollution, generating that necessary economic added value to the costs of the infrastructure transformation. Even with the incorporation of the consensus and favour of the public administration since the initial project formulations around the end of the 1990s, uncertainties still endure today around the actual benefits and costs that the implementation of the proposal would entail. It is calculated that the construction of the dock and the infrastructure reform could have a bearing on the costs of the surface to be built, calculated at about two thousand Euros per square metre – a premium considered too high with respect to the actual real estate values.

The alternative is the dike. The dike is reassuring in economic terms, even though it is difficult to manage because of traffic and urban settlement. Without being able to resolve the problem of the separation between the neighbourhoods to the north and the south, streets and railways, channelled into the existing trench of over two hundred metres in width, would continue to cut through the centre of the area. Reduced to about half the surfaces that could be built, the development of the area and its aspirations to become a dynamic and attractive metropolitan area would be drastically weakened. Leaving the infrastructures uncovered would not even contain the atmospheric and sound pollution, thus preventing the homes and services from being located near the trench itself.

Zuidas, with the WTC, Mahler 4, Gershwin, and River quarter sections, is built beside or above Highway A10 and the high-velocity train track for practical reasons, without any pretension to demonstrativeness or to the avant-garde look of Euralille. It is built simply where the ground, a precious and non-renewable resource, is already eroded and compromised. And it reconstitutes that sprawl, already cut up by road networks, attempting to capitalize economically on a real estate added value for a return from the operating of a new infrastructure development. Offices, homes, services, and commerce for over a million square metres foster one of the largest city sections under construction in Europe today, involving banking and insurance groups and multinational investment funds. A hybrid city mixes infrastructures, towers, and surfaces with the city block, a principle of urban settlement that relates the compact city of Berlage to the open building districts of Van Eesteren. The hyper-urban style, fostered by freely competing architectural signatures, is mixed with neopastoral forms in the gardens, along the allées containing plants, and in the artificial lakes. As often happens, here, too, opposing models accelerate in an urban pluralist design theme, open to the market of metropolitan traditions and, at the same time, to the aspirations of suburban life.

**Amsterdam**, Zuidas

Urban planning and coordination: DRO, Zuidas Amsterdam Development Office
Development company: Zuidas Amsterdam Development Corporation
Planning and implementation: 1998–ongoing

 1 World Trade Center: KPF
 2 Zuidplein
 3 ABN Amro: Pei Cobb Freed & Partners
 4 Offices: R. Viñoly
 5 Offices: T. Ito
 6 Uffici: SOM
 7 The Baker & McKenzie House: M. Graves
 8 Offices: F. van Dongen
 9 Offices: E. van Egeraat
10 Offices: UNStudio
11 Symphony: De Architekten Cie

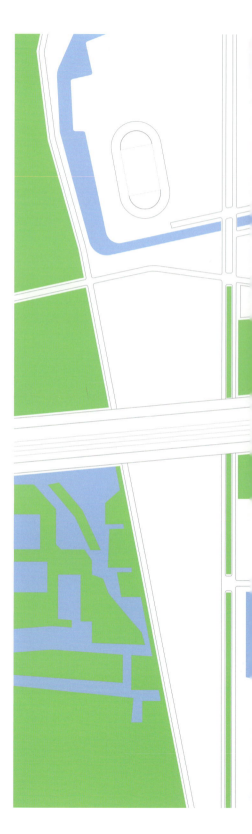

1
2

# Barcelona, Vila Olimpica, Forum 2004

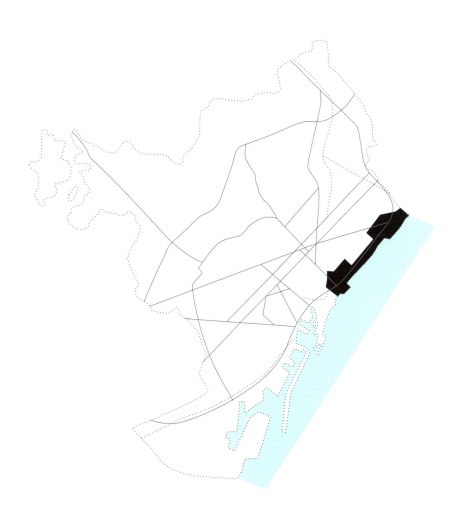

Concurrent with the administrative reorganization that began in 1979, and with the institution of the Corporació Metropolitana de Barcelona, a general rethinking is taking place about Barcelona and the role it plays in the conurbation that has grown around it. The demands for renewal aim to make Barcelona a capital of the Mediterranean. To this end, a strategic plan has been launched. Leaving behind the expansion previsions of the General Plan of 1976, there has been a certain amount of theoretical agitation erupting over the years in Europe, which, as an alternative to urban expansion, has called for the reconstruction of the city onto itself. The politics of *urbanismo estratégico*, advocated by Oriol Bohigas (director of planning of the city of Barcelona from 1980 to 1984), counts on timely implementations, capable of triggering the regeneration of the surrounding sections in a "healthy sort of 'metastasis' within the urban fabric" (1985). *Recuperation*, the strategy put into practice, acts on more fronts, and, within the work processes, envisages an alternating of different scales of renewal intervention. At the beginning, the urban revitalization of small spaces in the heart of the Ciutat Vella involved a micro-urban scale of work. Later on, partial infrastructure reorganizing affected public transit, and thus peripheral areas of the Ensanche and the oldest suburb were retrieved as collective spaces.

When the urban plan, so launched, was grafted onto the 1985 program for the 1992 Olympics, the scope and aim of the operations changed. An *idea-fuerza* was imposed that called for the multiple themes linked to the Olympic events – namely, new accessibility, new services and reception structures, new sports and recreational facilities – to become an integral part of a larger renewal and remodernization activity that would be capable of suggesting a new image for the city and also be used in the magnified system of the media. "The Olympics last fifteen days but the city lasts forever," stated Barcelona Mayor Maragall. The elation of being in the limelight and the will to victory of a city that, for decades, had to close in upon itself dictated the changing of the early slogan from *recuperation* to *innovation*. Recognizing in the urban plan the operating method for acting on an "intermediate scale," between the morphology of the city and the real embodiment of spaces and buildings, is in opposition to extreme forms of planning deregulation. Instead of instituting extreme forms of planning deregulation, a strategy that starts with concrete plans for effectively channelling resources and opportunities is able to win back the sea and overhaul the infrastructure system by rethinking the *forma urbis* in relation to the metropolitan scale.

The 1985 strategic plan promoted by J. Busquets identifies twelve "new centralities," conceived as truly complex and articulated city segments, where, among other functions, one could locate the Olympic facilities as well. The "new centralities" are related and interconnected with each other by the Rondes, link roads that the rearrangement of the Cinturones creates, using urban criteria, so as to be configured as itineraries within the city and, together, permit easy accessibility.

In establishing a relationship between the hill of Montjuïc and the industrial zone of the Poblenou, the problem of the reconversion of the waterfront emerges, channelling the city's energies towards the sea. Powerfully and boldly, the plan overturns a centuries-old rejection of the waterfront, which Cerdà, by forcing expansion towards the hinterland, had already subordinated, and on which, over the course of the twentieth century, the city would turn its back, allocating at the waterfront the great industrial area linked to the railway and the port.

In 1984, under the plan initiated by M. de Solà, the Moll de la Fusta, along with the first stretch of the Ronda Litoral, was completed. This process of transformation, in less than twenty years, converted around six kilometres of sea and shore, from Montjuïc towards Barceloneta, for the Vila Olimpica and the tourist harbour, for the Parque of the Litoral and Poblenou and their beaches, up until the development operations of the Diagonal mar, the Esplanade of the Forum 2004, and the rehabilitation of the estuary of the Besòs River. These developments provided the city with a public and landscape space unequalled in Europe, comparable, in terms of urban and environmental value and openness and collective values, only to the great works of Roosevelt, when Moses brought New York onto the beaches of Long Island.

A long process was then initiated, guided by principles of an urban town planning that proved to be truly creative in providing stable characteristics to the overall urban structure. In 1985, the MBMP studio begins to plan the Vila Olimpica, for which they reserved a strategic role in the transformation of Barcelona. A key element for the redesign of the waterfront necessarily entailed the reorganization of the infrastructure system along the coast, striving for compatibility with the urban settlement, and the revival of a part of the city, where a joint presence of functions, forms, and open spaces offers true liveability in accordance with contemporary expectations. The development of such a complex part of the city saw the urban project tackling crucial issues in the reorganization process. From conception to completion, it is necessary to analyze the control of balances between urban continuity and building variety, between the existing city and the new arrangement, along with the revitalization of the "urban traditions" in view of contemporary user demands, as well as the management of the conflicts between suburban infrastructures and urban utilization of the spaces. The Vila Olimpica represents one of the first contemporary experiments in "coordinated urban planning." Its capabilities have been tested. Its potential, consequences, and limits have been scanned. Having proved its effectiveness as a working tool, it has led to abundant sequels in Europe.

With the willingness to go along with and transcribe the inherited "traditions" of the city of the past, the morphological proposals for the Vila Olimpica reconnect to the unrest over critical revision of modern urban planning, the as yet unfinished experience of Iba 84 in Berlin, and the theoretical contributions of the "movement for city reconstruction." The public space becomes a stable and lasting reality to which the new urban identity can be anchored. The city block, reinterpreted by the revisionism of Bohigas, represents the midway element that allows for the construction of individual building lots to be entrusted to different designers.

The morphological-type option is intertwined with the need to radically reorganize the infrastructures that cut and separate the city from the sea. The conception of the whole lets itself be guided by the specificities of the space: the regular routes of the Ensanche give birth to new city blocks. The sinuous line of the coastline becomes the matrix of the linear park connected to the Ronda. The railway junction becomes the border of the new urban settlement on the Parque de la Ciutadella. The view onto the horizon directs one towards the *palazzata a mare* (the row of multiple story homes that line the seashore) on the Parque del Litoral. The structure of the layout, in the renewed tradition of the City Beautiful, keeps in balance the urban demands, supported by the plan of the Ensanche and the design of the new infrastructures that celebrate environmental merits – a physical and conceptual substratum that interconnects urban layout, infrastructure reorganization, landscape, and construction. Guidelines focus the work of about thirty architects, including Amadó & Domènech, Boffill, Piñón & Viaplana, Bach & Mora, Lapeña & Torres, Bonell & Rius, and Tusquets, with a goal to produce a controlled variety, counterpoint to a predominant morphological uniformity.

An urban area, for years relegated to the presence of inhabitants and tourists, must now work hard to compete with the new appeals and strengths found along the coast, compared to the new urban transformation models launched on the occasion of the 2004 Universal Forum of Cultures. Situated to the north of the Poblenou along the Diagonal, between Plaça Glòries and the confluence with the Riu Besòs, the large urban project of the Forum 2004 marks a change in the urban policies of the municipality of Barcelona. From 1998, notwithstanding the Plan General Metropolitano, these policies comply with the tendency towards leverage planning, brought to Continental Europe from Anglo-Saxon culture, introduce criteria of greater flexibility, and resort to the practice of "case by case" negotiations. To compensate for the lack of public financing, private capital is attracted for the processes of urban transformation, some coming from foreign countries and channelled into real estate investments made economically attractive. The change of scale in the shift from city to metropolis, indispensable for the global competition in investments, pushes towards an emphasis on specific uses – including conferences, exhibitions, businesses, and receptions – in order to situate Barcelona in the marketplace for international attractions, strengthening its propensity as a touristy city.

The 2004 Universal Forum of Cultures represents, like the previous Olympics, an opportunity and a stimulus to redevelop marginalized and depressed parts of the city and, at the same time, a moment of reflection on a general renewal of the urban image. But if past years have envisioned a redevelopment of the city in continuity with existing urban values, with the Forum 2004 the frame of reference also changed. The obligatory reference now goes to the already widespread and predominating inclination to launch urban reforms by preparing events with international resonance, whose media success would attract the commercial and real estate success of the development operation – a success, however, to which several factors contribute, including the inclusion of new and surprising functions, the mixing of different practices and prospects for their enjoyment, and, last but not least, the unique use of architectural signatures.

The new city section, wending its way along the sea, appears as a collection of different developments, each of which originates from a particular urban settlement theme. An empirical approach supports the destructuring initiated by the clash between the sudden highway splitting of the Ronda Litoral and the regular design of the branches of the Ensanche. City segments and landscapes  "in collision," Colin Rowe (1978) would say, where a host of representations in competition present a *generic landscape* of towers, "top plates," artificial land, gardens, and interchanges, flourish among new and old infrastructures. The floating Forum of Herzog & de Meuron and, like a harbour infrastructure, the long Convention Centre of Mateo appear on the edges of the Esplanade of Lapeña and Torres, spreading for twenty hectares like a gigantic origami leaf. Behind, to mark the entrance to the Diagonal, the towers of KPF rise up from the park of Miralles and Tagliabue, triangulating the horizontal continuity of the Ensanche, with the Agbar tower of J. Nouvel in Plaça Glòries and those of Som and Ortiz.Leon to the Vila Olimpica. A rare and enlarged empty space, partially covered by impressive canopied terraces serve as the geometric and symbolic hub of the area and support the photovoltaic energy plant. Detached land chunks, split by infrastructure markings, "top plates" slowly going adrift, ruffled and corrugated by plant or mineral dunes, become connected by artificial esplanades in the Auditoria Park by Foa and in the Bathing area by B. Galì, or pass over infrastructures and building obstacles in the Parque of the Litoral northeast by Abalos & Herreros, the parterre garden of the large incineration plant rising to the level of a technical monument.

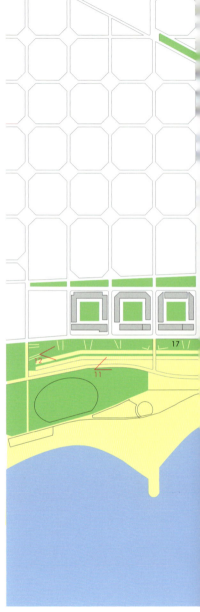

**Barcelona**, Vila Olimpica, Forum 2004

*Vila Olimpica*
Urban planning and coordination: MBMP
Development company: Nova Icària SA
Planning and implementation: 1985–1994

*Diagonal Mar*
Urban planning and coordination: KPF
Development company: Hines
Planning and implementation: 1999–2004

*Forum 2004*
Urban planning and coordination: Josep Acebillo
Planning and implementation: 1999–2004

1 City block: MBMP
2 City block: Correa & Milà
3 City block: Bonell & Rius
4 City block: Piñón & Viaplana
5 City block: Lapeña & Torres
6 City block: Tusquets & Diaz
7 Eurocity: Amadó & Domènech
8 Eurocity: Piñón & Viaplana
9 Eurocity: Piñón & Viaplana
10 Eurocity: Piñón & Viaplana
11 Central Telefonica: Bach & Mora
12 Hotel Arts Tower: SOM
13 Mapfre Tower: Ortiz.Léon
14 Weather centre: A. Siza
15 Parque del Litoral: MBMP
16 Port Olimpic, MBMP
17 Ronda del Litoral Promenade: Ravetllat Mira & Ribas Seix
18 Forum: Herzog & de Meuron
19 CCIB: MAP Arquitectos
20 Hotel Diagona: O. Tusquets
21 Diagonal Mar shopping centre: R. Stern
22 Parque Diagonal Mar: Miralles & Tagliabue EMBT
23 Esplanade: Lapeña & Torres
24 Parc dels Auditoris: FOA
25 Bathing area: B. Galí
26 Parque del Litoral nord-est: Abalos y Herreros

17
18

# Berlin, Potsdamer Platz

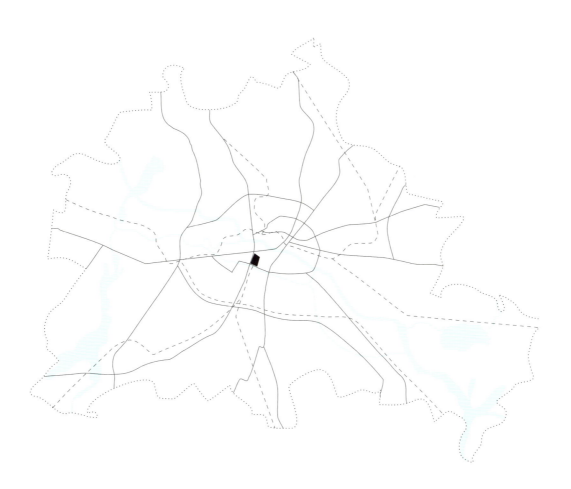

After the fall of the Berlin Wall in 1989, the perspective of a reunified Berlin, once again the German capital, became the reason for rethinking the city in relation to its parts, and for finding more places of centrality within it. After the Wall was built in 1961, the geometric and symbolic core of Berlin became one of the Wall's victims, confined to the margins of the city among the defaced edges of the chessboard of Frederick II, the barely perceptible traces of the famous baroque icons of Leipziger Platz and Pariser Platz, and the abandoned lands along the border, interspersed with interrupted streets and tracks. For years, the Wall marked a division – two cities struggled to build two opposite centres in competition with each other. West Berlin would comply with the centuries-old tendency to urban growth and endorse the direction towards Charlottenburg. East Berlin would deploy the banners of the new power towards Alexanderplatz and along the Stalinallee. Allocating new centres constituted the right to a reconstruction that in reality wished to be seen as a new foundation, which meant the physical elimination of memories. These intentions were already made explicit in 1946, as elaborated in the general plan, the *Kollektivplan*, directed by Hans Scharoun.

In the early 1990s, the centre of the newly unified city was a vast empty space that, for thirty years, had been the back of the two cities: a topological centre permeated with absences that left behind city sections in conflict, the result of fragmentary designs and interrupted plans. It would be these empty spaces that would advocate the putting into practice of principles of "densification" aimed at eliminating the signs of conflict and recent history. As opposed to what happened during the postwar reconstruction, the eradications went on in the name of an imagined history, rather than future desires, with a generalized type of building rather than demolitions.

The operation, echoing Iba 84 (International Building Exhibition Berlin), reawakened enthusiasms, pointing to the rebirth of a new laboratory *en plein air* for architecture and urban planning in the Berlin of the 1990s. Principles and methods fell into unhealthy contradictions. The will to innovation, followed by international competitions, conflicted with the restoration rules of urban composition. Transformed into law in the Planwerk, rules of Kritische Rekonstruktion in fact gave place to compromises and solutions that were not always equal to the exceptional nature of the spaces. The reconstructions around the Brandenburg Gate, the completions to Friedrichstrasse, the new "political city" with the Reichstag on the bay of the Spree, the redevelopment of the Potsdamer area, and the expected changes to Alexanderplatz and the Spreeinsel lacked a conscious strategy for the city's modernization and exposed the occasional exploitation in the urban centre of "abandoned" areas, to which public investments and private capital were channelled. With clear-headedness, Osvald Mathias Ungers, who had studied the city at length and made plans for it, asked himself, "Does there exist a plan for Berlin, or is it reduced to something half-baked, to an ad hoc way of working half-heartedly, to a program adopted by acclamation according to the ideological and economic situation of the moment or of personal preference? … a do-it-yourself of images, from wherever they may come, be it from Italy or Manhattan?" (*Lotus* 80).

The incoherence of the rules leaves the field open to dissension, as is evident in the letter that Rem Koolhaas wrote to the Frankfurter *Allgemeine Zeitung* on October 16, 1991 as a comment on the debate unleashed during the award ceremony for the Potsdamer/Leipziger Platz competition: "From the beginning, projects rich in intelligence, and enterprising potential, and able to convey new urban visions have been excluded to the benefit of projects considered 'normal' … that all reveal the same weaknesses because they are still bound to classic nineteenth-century morphology based on the city block."

Pursuing the image of a Berlinische Architektur with themes derived from the Kritische Rekonstruktion, Hilmer & Sattler won the competition for the Potsdamer/Leipziger Platz master plan in 1991. City blocks, carved from the existing streets or from restored historic routes, are interspersed with clearings and parterre gardens: the dictates of urban beautification cannot configure a true urban fabric, nor can they demand relations with the surrounding city and with the pertinent transit infrastructures. The unresolved incompatibilities would compromise the developments, even though the subsequent contest projects tried to lessen the more pernicious effects.

The Senate's decision to implement the master plan with three competitions set up by the proprietors of the areas, and to be autonomously convened without any general coordination, further fragmented the whole. With each operation centred on itself, on the scale of a city section coinciding with the company image, Sony, Debis, and Abb produced identities and recognizable traits, each one separate and lacking any affiliation to another. Potsdamer Strasse represents a separation and a border between segments endowed with their own character and individuality: a differentiation device between competitors who operate on the real estate market and on urban systems, offering comparable products of diverse forms and themes. Potsdamer Platz thus divested of its functions and urban values is merely a geometric fusion of the vibrant perimeters of the corner buildings.

More than the others, the 1992 plan of the Murphy/Jahn studio for Sony expresses a type of self-referentiality. The street volumes are expressed in exclusive terms, starting from the currents generated by flow rates and following the dictates of retail planning and totally independent of the Tiergarten, similar to the Debis development. Having submitted to the dictates of the Kritische Rekonstruktion, the structural layout and the architecture agreed to display a unified procedure, bringing together a perimeter of buildings aligned along the streets with the central structure of an elliptical arcade. There are two hubs: Peter Walker's thematic garden, on the level of urban recreation, wends its way with twists and turns between the ground floor and the underground floors, between the public halls and entertainment sites; the other, the tower in Potszdamer Platz, with the stripped skin of its transparent facades, stands out like a landmark in the urban landscape, evoking an intangible and light world, chosen connotations emblematic of the Japanese brand in the city.

In 1993, Giorgio Grassi won the competition for the Abb area, rejecting the imitation of the city block proposed by the master plan. He proposed the formation of blocks in the shape of a C and an H, opening onto the street and the garden. Instead of being based on the city block as an element of urban definition, the formation is a morphological-type option, based metaphorically on the building principles of certain sections of late baroque and neoclassical Berlin, such as the Ehemalige Wilhelmstrasse. It evokes the deep structures of the city as an element of resistance to the recent developments to Potsdamer Platz, considered a reproduction of an image of urban character, with a superficial focus. The widespread split between heroic expectations and the "normality" of the outcome causes one to interpret the simplifications implemented on the historical structures as heralds of similarities rather than differences, with respect to Hilmer & Sattler.

Certainly a coordinated effort would not have generated separate enclaves, even though Renzo Piano, for the Debis area, formulated a coordinated plan and, within the limitations of the preconditions, was able to give life to a relatively diverse and well-structured city section. When, in 1992, Piano, together with Kohlbecker, won the competition, he modified the master plan with pragmatism: from rational modifications, from diversified practices and traditions, a less abstract urban character would emerge, even within the sphere of a simulation. The city made up of blocks, as stipulated by the building norms according to the tradition of Kritische Rekonstruktion, becomes blended with the "downtown" model that had already been proposed by previous competition projects for the Potsdamer/Leipziger Platz, in as much as this model was more suitable to the role of Berlin as capital city and to the new extent of real estate investments. On the edges of the area, the city blocks project upwards and are composed of towers and corner buildings that respond to the surrounding urban reality and symbolically point out the significance of a unified identity. This "unity," an indispensable requisite of identity and brand recognition within the logic of economic competition, would have to be balanced with the contrasting character of "variety," an inescapable trait of a city, and of that ready-made urban character, able to guarantee an immediate marketability.

The planimetric, volumetric, and structural composition of the whole layout and the single building parts are controlled together, with pragmatism and confidence, through the coordination of different architects. Everything that in the running of other coordinated urban projects would have been revealed as functional and profitable is immediately incorporated and introduced into the project's production structure. Alignments, building parts, and uniformity of materials and building systems are simple rules, assigned to Koolhoff, Kohlbecker, Moneo, Isozaki, Rogers, Lauber & Wöhr, with the intention of assembling spatial sequences within a cohesive "building fabric." These "architectures," planned and built by Piano himself, play a game of counterpoint between opacity and clarity, rule and exception, and allude to the city of the past, alternating between "monument and fabric," which the varieties of surfaces and volumes reproduce thematically.

The open-space project is invaluable for conferring a coherent whole and a certain effect of urban expansiveness. Piano redefines the proportions between the height of the buildings and the width of the street. He specifies in detail the architectural elements of the grounding of the buildings. He designs the elements that give special character to the open spaces, reproducing the materials and the details of the historic centre. He offers up destinations and transparencies by enlarging the urban space right into the halls of the buildings.

In Piano's "townscape," it is the visual and perceptive approach that guides the juxtaposition and the search for the syntax between buildings: he creates panoramas and partial views; he assembles in sequence the harmony of volumes and spaces. With such "frames," Piano gathers the buildings of other architects into a close relationship with his own, or he emphasizes in a spectacular way an angle or a vertical line, or he sets, for the sake of contrast, the tectonic building of Koolhoff against the *misiano* dematerialization of his wrapped towers.

The "visible" approach builds a varied unity even in the choice of recurring materials. It is not the materials that prevail, but the visible effects of a "light" building process, of a dry assemblage of consecutive industrialized elements. The materials are formed in grids, bi-dimensional lattices, perforated panels that Piano, Rogers, and Isozaki use to obtain fade-outs, transparencies, and shadings to enhance perceptual and environmental values. This contributes to the suggestion of the whole: a "city staging" that, in a kind of urban incident, delivers itself from the solidity of the "Berlin of stone." Only Kollhoff and Moneo, reluctant to accept such principles, resist this approach. By comparison, their buildings evoke a typological entrenchment and a tectonic solidity, aspiring towards a Neue Berlinische Architektur.

**Berlin**, Potsdamer Platz

*DeBis*
Urban planning and coordination: Renzo Piano, Christoph Kohlbecker
Development company: Debis
Planning and implementation: 1993–2000

*Sony Center*
Urban and architectural planning: Murphy/Jahn
Development company: Sony
Planning and implementation: 1996–2000

*Park Kolonnaden*
Urban planning and coordination: Giorgio Grassi
Development company: Abb
Planning and implementation: 1996–2002

1 Tower: R. Piano, C. Kohlbecker
2 Business center: H. Kollhoff
3 Debis center: R. Piano, C. Kohlbecker
4 Musical theatre Casinò: R. Piano, C. Kohlbecker
5 Grand Hyatt: R. Moneo
6 Mercedes-Benz: Center: R. Moneo
7 City block: Lauber & Wöhr
8 Imax: R. Piano, C. Kohlbecker
9 City blocks: R. Piano
10 Arkaden: R. Piano
11 Berliner Volksbank: A. Isozaki
12 City blocks on the Linkstrasse: R. Rogers
13 Sony Center: Murphy/Jahn
14 Offices and businesses: Schweger & Partner
15 Offices, G. Grassi: J. Sawade
16 Offices and residence: Diener & Diener
17 Bahnhof Potsdamer Platz: Hilmer & Sattler
18 Tilla-Durieux Park: DS Landschapsarchitecten
19 Ritz Carlton Hotel: Hilmer & Sattler
20 Delbrück-Haus: H. Kollhoff
21 Staatsbibliothek: H. Scharoun
22 Philharmonie: H. Scharoun
23 Tiergarten

# **Breda**, Chassé Park

Since the middle of the 1980s, upon relaunching the city into the trade fair and convention market of the entertainment and service sectors, the municipal administration of Breda has been initiating industrial regeneration programs, closely associated with residential policies, to tackle the issues of the increase in retirees and the arrival of new inhabitants who have been attracted by economic opportunities resulting from changed work and social conditions. Within this context, the idea to redevelop the Chassé Terrain, once a property under military auspices, began to evolve in 1994. The project was entrusted to OMA, which availed itself of the landscape consultancy of West 8.

Now a revitalized part of the city, Chassé Park along with Parksport, to Wilhelmina Park and the Brabant, forms a green-loop, a clearly visible green system within the icon of the *forma urbis*, which provides the city with specific environmental values and those of integration of landscape and city structures. A well-constructed arrangement of housing and open spaces extends over fourteen hectares. Nine hundred dwellings – luxury apartments, rental housing, subsidized housing, and residences for seniors and the disabled – are interwoven with offices, new community spaces, and existing public buildings whose value the project enhanced, including the town hall from the 1970s, the Chassé Theater from the 1980s by Hertzberger, certain military buildings from the early nineteenth century and renovated to include Breda's Museum en Archief in the Kloosterkazerne, the new Holland Casino, and the Mezz Muziekcentrum.

The urban settlement model is the *campus*. If the ideal space around which buildings achieve a greater figurative representation is, in the European city of the past, the square, in the modern city it is often the park that organizes and arranges the city structures in groupings, independent but interconnected at the same time. In the transition from the paradigm of the square to that of the park, new connective freedoms between buildings are mobilized along with their new possibilities of connection with infrastructures and urban spaces. For OMA, the campus, besides being the morphological principle that reunites and arranges buildings that are different from each other because of special architectural and typological characteristics, represents the chance to pay attention to today's aspirations and different dwelling styles. The dichotomy between artifice and nature, sealed by the heroic vision of Le Corbusier in the housing model of the Unité, disintegrates here in the mixing of heterogeneous elements distributed in such a way as to form a "continuous environment." An ecological dimension is sought. There is an aspiration to reach some sort of *climax* in which the urban structures, the natural elements, the traditions and the way of life, in all their disparate meanings, may be able to find a new balance. Even the buildings would seem to aspire to belong to such an ecosystem in that they are able to express the character and composition of the natural object, and therefore have a true environmental value: in this tension, they establish a connection with Le Corbusier's Immeubles-Villas and the Roq and Rob housing developments.

With the increased quantity of existing trees, there is a continuous forest of oaks and two wide clearings to form the new city section: the Chassé Promenade and the Court Carré of Breda's Museum. This is an unmistakable landscape architecture approach: the placement of the buildings and their connection to each other are brought back to the principles of landscape planning, and the conventional norms of urban planning are thrown into disorder. In tackling this theme of urban settlement, OMA does not limit itself to disassociating building and space, as in the modernist tradition. In an innovative context, no longer square or street but park, it inserts design themes of urban composition, perspective visuals, axiality, and relationships between parts. The collage-like matrix that Colin Rowe in "Collage City" finds in Roman Forums, in Acropolises, and in the rest of the imperial villas and Hellenic cities opens here into an interweaving of airy relationships, frees up the relationship between architecture and space, which does not lack for the picturesque in the fortuitous vistas.

Thoughtful placement strategies allow the new to interact with the old and with the city on its borders. The visual play thus enacted empirically finds continuously perfectible formations: visual targets and perceptual routes pierce the area and transform it into an aperture, porous and permeable to accesses and crossings. To virtually continue the axis route of the Molenstraat, as it exits the historic centre, is the empty space of the Chassé Promenade, a paved esplanade in the centre of the park. Distortions, misalignments, and rotations force the gaze from the buildings to alight on the Gothic spire of the Grote Kerk. And in order to open a visual channel onto Wilhelmina Park, the buildings, without hesitation, are cut into and made to take on unusual designs. The wish is to moderate the enclave character, derived from the development model and the ecosystem of functions, so that the settlement can open onto a fluid and pervasive spatiality, allowing itself to be crossed, by planned routes and well-thought-out visual limits, from the surrounding city.

This project involves different architects for different buildings. Even in their distinct architectural and formal individuality, the buildings manage to maintain moments of interconnection with existing structures and the surrounding city, transcending the simple morphological continuity: they are autonomous but enclosed in a relational logic in articulated and differentiated wholes, so as to stay sensitive to mutual demands and the interacting of partnerships. The proximity approach measures benefits and consistencies of ties and reciprocal affinities: in a strategic use of the proximities, it controls alignments and rotations, and tests the compatibility of distances and introspections. Relational balances, reached through consecutive trials and corrections, govern the dynamics of attractions and rejections, circumscribing fields of equivalent forces.

Something has radically changed. The project coordination, a surveillance tool to limit deformities and inequalities and to achieve a varied but predicted homogeneity, gives way to coordination as a control of possibilities – an open management of the possibilities that knows and wishes to celebrate differences within occasionally constructed horizons of belonging. If it is no longer well-known urban models that provide the rules of connecting – alignments, the heights of the eaves, the *ordonnance* – the legitimacy of methods and forms of coexistence between the different buildings, between open spaces and flow, between function and tradition is to be sought in the project's construction process and justified only by the value of the outcome.

Perceptual stratifications of the constructed volumes and the controlled variety of architectural languages and materials offer, along the way, changing frameworks of the landscape model, rather than the urban one. Pieces of urban complexity, sometimes that of a metropolis, are carved out instead within the buildings, formed into complex morphological organisms. The experimenting with different housing methods brings together a sample collection of "microcosms," rooted in disparate city models reconciled in the idyllic dimension of the landscape. We have the Team X metropolis cluster matrix in the towers of De Geyter, the urban city block of the Carré by OMA, the use of infill by Van Sambeek, the low-rise compact urban fabric of Van Veen, Kollhoff's Het paleis that epitomizes the theme of the "institutionalization" of housing, and the hybrid block of the Van der Torre residence.

Following the path of the modern tradition of the Universal Exhibitions of Architecture, the development of a city section becomes, as in the Stuttgart Weissenhof, the Milan Qt8, and the Interbau 57 in Berlin, a place to reflect more fully on different housing methods. But the experimentation of Chassé Park is not concerned with a housing typology: it is not interested in creating "housing cells," as in the modern heroic period, nor is it interested in investigating aggregate aspects, like the exponents of Team X and the Metabolist movement were doing. What prevails instead is the intention to envisage different residential "worlds" and multiple housing themes within a scenario of coexistence. After the 1960s and 1970s, and having abandoned that welfare state model that was responding to the housing emergency with mass-housing neighbourhoods, in Chassé Park, the tendency was toward a society modelled on desire – a collage that was not only morphological but answered various residential aspirations. Chassé Park represents this collage not so much for the architectural language adopted, but more for the disparate combinations of dwellings – an available standard – with connection buffers, elements of transition between the inside and the outside, areas of communication between vehicular accessibility and access concourses, between public *prolongement du logis* and the privacy of the apartment. These new perspectives demand a greater complexity between indoors and outdoors, without preventing reflection upon the internal space of the building and its unique architectural individuality. With new passion and enthusiasm, and with different results, the lesson of the great masters – Alvar Aalto, Mies van der Rohe, Le Corbusier, and later Albini, Gardella, Coderch, Martin, Lasdun – become reinstated, often, in the experiences of "critical reconstruction," to dissolve into an exclusive attention towards urban morphology.

Just as the nineteenth-century urban parks succeeded in absorbing and adapting those infrastructures that were considered incompatible with urban structures and functions, the park here represents a powerful means for controlling the parking areas and the vehicle access flow to the homes. The different types of parking formations and a careful management of vehicle circulation manage to keep the dynamic fluidity and meet the environmental standards of contemporary habitability. One arrives at home by car in the open air, avoiding the suspension or annihilation of the landscape experience through the darkness of a tunnel or an underground route.
A significant example of creativity, energizing the entire development at the metropolis level, is the large public parking area, the centre of gravity of the park, and the link between the new residential buildings and the existing public buildings. The beneficial overlay of the bucolic view of buildings within the landscape and the dynamics of a metropolis is demonstrated by the architectural quality of this gathering place. The usual site of a parking lot on the outer edges is here reversed and given the importance of a large public space for eight hundred cars. A space filled with urban vitality, open and well-lit, similar to the mezzanine floors of the subway (metro) or to other concourses of train stations, it accommodates service facilities and commercial spaces and allows one to directly access the underground entrances to the public buildings. It is precisely all these functions that establish its success, thus fulfilling the project's expectations. Paradoxically, it is one of the liveliest and busiest places in town.

Large and generously bright atriums contain the stairways to the roof: a great "market place" whose tri-dimensional geometries formed in grey stone are linked to the positioning of the surrounding gardens. This is an immeasurable space, hovering between a geographical reality and an unusual urban space, to whose ambivalence of forms and plurality of functions is added the value of the necessary infrastructure – the theme and intention of the development as a whole.

**Breda**, Chassé Park

Urban planning and coordination: OMA-Rem Koolhaas
Landscape plan: West 8
Development company: Chassépark
Planning and implementation: 1995–2012

 1 Chassé Promenade: West 8; Parking: OMA
 2 Theatre houses: T. van Esch
 3 Cluster: X. De Geyter
 4 Park: P. Blaisse
 5 Carré Building: OMA
 6 Residence: van Sambeek & van Veen
 7 Het Paleis: H. Kollhoff
 8 Patio villas: van Sambeek & van Veen
 9 Winter Garden apartments: D. van der Torre
10 Mezz Muziekcentrum: E. van Egeraat
11 Breda's Museum
12 Chassé Theater: H. Hertzberger
13 Kloosterkazerne

1
2

# **Hamburg**, HafenCity

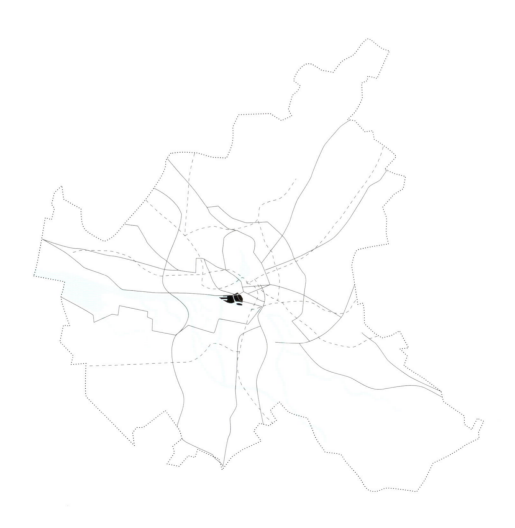

The decision made in 1997 by the Bürgerschaft to build HafenCity, a new urban centre in the decommissioned harbour areas, caused lively debates in the city and provoked dissatisfaction among those who believed that an urban operation of such transformation and development, which corresponded to 40 percent of the existing city, was overambitious. There would be two and a half million square metres of surface to build upon and more than ten kilometres of waterfront. Furthermore, the proposed centre was in the southern part of the city, which was historically perceived as less liveable and attractive because of the prevalence of harbour, industrial, and wholesale business activities. But Hamburg, a city-state in the centre, with its seven districts of a metropolitan area of over four million inhabitants, wanted to take on this challenge precisely because of the reconversion of the logistic systems moved towards the sea, a fact that confirmed its role as one of the largest container terminals in the world but, at the same time, left large portions of the old port in disuse.

The master plan conceived by Kees Christiaanse/ASTOC, winner of the international competition, announced in 1998 to solicit project ideas suited to the formation of the new centre, seems to blend together the precepts of New Urbanism with the principles of Kritische Rekonstruktion. City blocks, streets, squares, parks, gardens, high urban density with low-rise building – these ingredients were thought to generate a known and reassuring urban reality. The vision is that of a unified city, where the outline of the city block dominates and forms sinuous stretches of buildings that follow the path to the port basins and reinterpret the Speicherstadt, that splendid "city of bricks" made up of nineteenth-century warehouses. The design's structure, with its continuous and organic facades, creates intervals of linear parks, a sort of greenway wending its way along and flowing into the blueway of the port basins. The city's public space, in fact, continues onto the waters of the Elbe, which, as in the expansion operations conducted on the baroque city, becomes part of the urban scene and has been restored for the enjoyment of the inhabitants.

These principles of traditional urban planning, gleaned in a pragmatic and non-ideological way, are adaptable for reinterpretation in subsequent phases, beginning with the design process and then during construction. Additional themes have also emerged: the need to differentiate the morphology and typology of the buildings in relation to the functions, the problem of river water control, the issue of public and private transit, the principles of environmental sustainability, the saving of non-renewable resources, and the delivery time of the construction.

After the Bürgerschaft approved the competition project in 1999, project coordination and implementation occurred within the shared capital company of the HafenCity Hamburg GmbH, which answers directly to the municipality. In fact, the city of Hamburg continues to exert a strong supervisory power over the development process of this urban section as the holder of more than 90 percent of the areas involved, united under the special ownership of the city and the port (Stadt und Hafen). The development agency, besides superintending and coordinating the project phases, also manages the land development infrastructure and the assignment of areas to investors through open competitions in which project quality and the overall financial offer are simultaneously judged. Such a worthy process engenders private benefits for those investors who are not saddled with the risks, and even financial benefits connected with the uncertainties of approval or the market. There are public benefits as well, such as the forfeiture of the land revenues, which are redistributed through public works and an improved urban quality of life.

In the drafting of the urban plan and in subsequent operational phases, the initial unity of the master plan is articulated in twelve neighbourhoods. And this unity also happened by greatly respecting the specificity of the individual jetties and by maintaining part of the existing buildings when they communicated something of singular architectural or urban significance – the Kaispeicher A, for example, upon which the new Elbphilharmonie is being built, and the Kaispeicher B, which has been restored as the headquarters of the International Maritime Museum.

But an issue addressed in the conception of the whole, and constituting a determining factor for providing unity to the whole and to the articulation of its parts, concerns the strategic choice of elevating all the port wharves almost four metres and fixing the building floors at eight metres above river level. This decision was reached in order to protect the new city sector from possible increases in the water's height, and as an alternative to the construction of a perimeter dike, which would have acted as a physical and environmental barrier that would compromise the area's unique setting. A new artificial topography, upon which the city blocks and streets must rest, demands plans for buildings and open spaces that relate to the existing city and the bodies of water around it. Sandtorkai, the first neighbourhood built, in a more explicit way manifests the new land infrastructure theme. Eight building blocks, destined to be a mixture of residences and offices, rest on a continuous basement that contains parking lots and storage facilities, about four metres in height above the dock and the road coming from the city. To express this quality of suspension, the buildings create an unsymmetrical overhang, projecting towards the lake basin – a structural reinterpretation of the image of a harbour, hovering between bridge cranes and gigantic standing cranes. The single building blocks are planned by different architects who, by interpreting the themes suggested by the master plan in different ways, have expressed the various features, from infrastructure or macrostructures to the building features. As a whole, they form a relatively unified image within the building variety, so that dealing with the large space of the port basins is possible. From the uninterrupted basement, towards the existing city, bridges and boardwalks open out, creating a new pedestrian and cycling level, which then knits itself into the downtown street network, after having crossed the nearby Speicherstadt, allowing for evocative views at a medium height. Sandtorpark is conceived as an amalgam of city blocks formed around a central square. But the situation itself of an urban space built upon an artificial embankment, formed from the remains of land reclamations and opening onto the side towards the port basins, upsets the traditional typology of the square, and joins it to a manufactured artifact, somewhere between a port infrastructure and a landscape creation.

Dalmannkai more fully reinterprets the structure of the city block present in the master plan. The continuous basement, however, makes the relationship between the public promenade on the level of the docks and the semi-public spaces above them more complex and remarkable. The extreme edge of this neighbourhood is marked by the Elbphilharmonie, one of the most important public buildings in HafenCity. The Elbphilharmonie makes the city's inhabitants proud but, at the same time, its location, which some believe to be "off-centre," and its high costs have been contentious. Herzog & de Meuron, winners of the 2003 international competition, conceived this building as a vertical addition to the old harbour warehouse. By thrusting the imprint of the existing building upwards, they create a glass volume that smashes into the sky, as if disturbed by gusts of wind. Rising out of the Stadtkrone, it evokes memories of German expressionism based on the work of Bruno Taut or Hans Scharoun, and stands out like the Sidney Opera House by Utzon on the lower horizon of the harbour bay.

The Überseequartier also reinterprets the typology of the city block. Here it is not the infrastructure thematic that generates its developments as much as the will to build a shopping centre and an entertainment centre integrated with the city structure. The grand decision to conceive a diverse urban scene upon which to open the commercial ground floors of the city blocks creates an attractive city spot, and, similar to the Stadshart of Almere, prevents the inherent dangers in producing a shopping centre like a mono-functional macrostructure.

But it is the open spaces that most express the resolution between the infrastructure situation generated by the new urban height and the will to produce the morphology of the compact city. The resolution of the differences in height between the walkways along the basins and the areas on top of the city blocks occurs by arranging the public space into geometric complexes. Artificial terracing and sloping gardens accommodate staircases, boardwalks, and ramps that link up the different heights of the artificial topography. The method of formulating the open space layout here is different from similar harbour renewal operations of other German cities, such as Cologne, Düsseldorf, or Duisburg. In Hamburg, even with two Catalan landscape designers EMBT and B. Galì, the winners of architectural competitions for open spaces, it was desirable to bring in a piece of the Mediterranean, not only by importing landscape structures to modernize the entire image of the development but also by aspiring to create different lifestyles, more closely tied to the functioning of the city's open spaces, during the evening and the night. These would be the social rituals more common in Mediterranean cities than in those of northern Europe.

The renewal of the port of Hamburg seems to interweave two models: one adopted to redevelop the port of Amsterdam in terms of the morphological choice of the compact city, and the other adopted to renew the Barcelona seafront, with a tendency to mix urban layout and infrastructures in a new and better-formulated landscape vision. The same determination to unite more functions and collective traditions refers, even though in more moderate ways, to the festival marketplaces, in which the mix of functions, work spaces, and leisure spaces create a richer habitability. After all, the city of Hamburg has also known how to do that in past centuries, in its most select central sections, to which HafenCity is linked both physically and symbolically.

**Hamburg**, HafenCity

Urban planning and coordination: ASTOC
Architects & Planners, KCAP Architects & Planners
Development company: HafenCity Hamburg GmbH
Planning and implementation: 1997–ongoing

1 Elbphilharmonie: Herzog & de Meuron
2 Offices: Ingenhoven und Partner
3 Ocean's End: Böge-Lindner Architekten
4 H2O: Spengler-Wiescholek Architekten
5 Doks 4: Schweger Associated Architects
6 Residence: BRT Architekten
7 Harbour: M. Mathez
8 Residence: APB Architekten
9 Residence: J. Störmer
10 Amango: Böge-Lindner Architekten
11 Hamburg America Center: R. Meier
12 Katharinenschule: Spengler & Wiescholek
13 Offices: D. Chipperfield
14 The Oval: Ingenhoven und Partner
15 Residence: Böge-Lindner Architekten
16 Offices: Meurer Architekten
17 Residence: Schenk & Waiblinger Architekten
18 Residence: Spine 2, APB, KBNK architects
19 Residence: SML, SEHW
20 Residence: C. Lorenzen, KBNK architects, L. Winkler
21 Residence: PFP architekten
22 Residence, NPS Tchoban Voss
23 Coffee Plaza: R. Meier
24 Residence: KBNK architects, ASTOC Architects & Planners
25 Hafenliebe: Architekturbüro Neitmann
26 Commercial Center: Baumschlager Eberle
27 Kühne + Nagel: J. Störmer
28 SAP: Spengler & Wiescholek
29 Marco Polo Tower: Behnisch Architekten
30 Unilever Germany: Behnisch Architekten
31 Residential blocks: E. van Egeraat
32 Residential-commercial blocks: Trojan + Trojan, D. Joppien
33 Germanischer Lloyd: von Gerkan Marg und Partner, J. Störmer, Antonio Citterio and Partners
34 Ericus Contor: H. Larsen Architects
35 Spigel Group: H. Larsen Architects
36 Magellan terrassen: Miralles & Tagliabue EMBT
37 Sandorpark: Miralles & Tagliabue EMBT
38 Marco Polo terrassen: Miralles & Tagliabue EMBT
39 Magdeburger Hafen: B. Galí
40 Maritime Museum: Hanssen, Meerwein, MRLV Architekten

5

7
8

**Lille**, Euralille

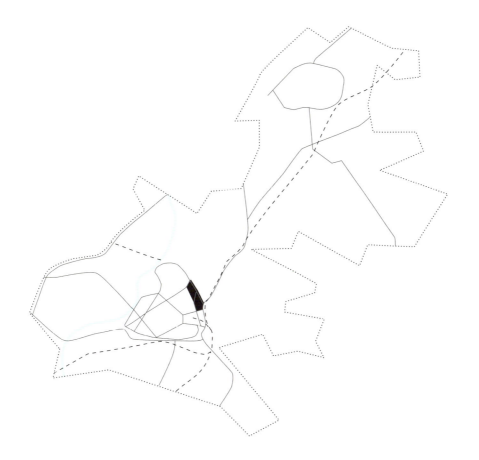

In Euralille, the approach more than the outcome provokes interest. Euralille represents a process, which from the very beginning, was continuously governed by its initiation process; a policy oriented towards correlating the city and its conurbation to an economic and social revival on an international level; an innovative mixture specified within the implementation itself of the operation, in the emphasis between the infrastructure complexities, program variations, and adjustments to goals; a conception of the contemporary city breaking with the city of the past.

The strategy of the project developed in synergy with urban policies, development management, and urban planning can be attributable to the partnership between three persons: Pierre Mauroy, mayor of Lille and president of the urban community; Jean-Paul Baïetto, director general of the Saem Euralille development agency; and Rem Koolhaas, author of the master plan and coordinator of the plans and operations.

It is necessary to go back to the 1986 official agreement between Margaret Thatcher and François Mitterrand that endorsed the will to uniting France and Great Britain with a tunnel under the English Channel and envisaged the Train à Grande Vitesse (TGV) as a fast transit link so that unexpected opportunities could be created for that polycentric urban community of the Nord-Pas de Calais region, which would be situated in the centre of the London–Paris–Brussels traffic flows. The economic and social advantages that a different interchange between local and continental traffic would bring did not escape the Lille community, governed by Pierre Mauroy. By virtue of his political influence as the former prime minister, Mauroy successfully persuaded Jacques Chirac, in December 1987, to make the lines of the northern European TGV pass right through the centre of the urban agglomeration of Lille, thus upsetting the programs that the rigid modelling of the SNCF (the state-owned railway company) had implemented, and envisaging its course for seventy kilometres to the airport interchange. The availability of some state property of 120 hectares east of Lille, between the ancient fortifications of Vauban and the open building development of Villeneuve d'Ascq, caused such a dynamic encounter between infrastructures and development as to incite Mauroy, at the beginning of 1988, to state, "There are rivers of highways and railroads so it is necessary to build a motor industry" (*L'architecture d'aujoud'hui*, 280).

Building a settlement in which one could anticipate a high quality of architecture and urban life – in other words, create the idea of an attractive city section – and fabricate it over the brief period of a decade, entailed implementing a particularly effective strategy: dissolving the bureaucratic chains of the Société d'économie mixte (SEM) and identifying new opportunities for an economic and financial montage that would be more suited to the goals. These are precisely the methods that have made possible the resulting success.

Creating conditions so that the implementation of an urban plan might reveal unprecedented opportunities and unusual urban visions becomes the primary objective and leads the way for the selection of a planner. Baïetto is convinced that "it is nonsense setting up an urban project by means of a competition: an urban project entails many elements, and therefore it is necessary to select the person rather than the project" (*L'architecture d'aujoud'hui*, 280). Thus, neither designs nor models were admitted to the consultation with the invited applicants. It was necessary to select the planner not the plan so that, through a relationship of negotiation with the clientele, the general master plan could be worked out, and other planners could be coordinated during the processing and implementation of the plan. In November 1998, Rem Koolhaas was unanimously chosen because he was the only one to propose an urban vision rather than project visions like the other competitors. Koolhaas, in this instance, demonstrated his aptitudes as an urban planner, ones that were verified by his reflections on the contemporary city, which had matured over time, and which found agreement with the clients' expectations. There were unique connections with the issues inherent in the development of Euralille: in particular, in the application of the theory of "Manhattanism," the thesis of a "culture of congestion," and the concept of the urban plan as a process, one to be regulated at the emergence of conflicts and problems.

"A project such as Euralille obligates one to make a metropolis," Rem Koolhaas (1988) asserted right from the beginning. And a metropolis plan is distinct from an urban plan: it insists on organizing the structural components of the city and the periphery together; it aspires to shape and confer an urban character on the structures and mechanisms conceived as an alternative and in antithesis to the city itself – the train stations, the malls, the business and exhibition centres, the mobility infrastructures.

At the beginning of 1989, in two workshops, OMA identified objectives that in the subsequent plans would be able to guide the morphological and program variations while still allowing free play: untying the "Gordian knot" of the existing infrastructures; physically and visibly express the relationship between TGV and city; and facilitate the crossing of the settlement by improving the fringes and interspaces. Fused to the programmatic elements, such objectives create a thematic classification gleaned from the imagery of the metropolis: the business centre as an accumulation of towers, the triangle between the stations as a mixed living surface, the convention centre as a macrostructural component, and the park as an artificial hill at the centre of the residential area. An "elemental montage" of Le Corbusier-style ascendency transcribes, in urban images, the grafting of intentions onto programs. "Simple" components, assembled in different formations, emphasize an interest in the "interconnection" between parts, more than for the parts themselves, and an attention towards the results of the "interaction" between programs rather than the programs themselves. Koolhaas imposes on the architects who are subsequently involved in the planning restrictive regulations on integration so as to chain infrastructures, buildings, and interspaces together – "thematic" chains or ones of "programmatic incest" but never structural chains. The paratactical composition uses a random surrealistic procedure of the *cadavre exquis* to urge the architects to produce freely competing "signature works of art." Perhaps this is the first case in which the plan and the "signature" of the planner give added value to a new city part. A collage-like accumulation – a collision of buildings and infrastructures, artificial and natural spaces – evokes congestion and density, but by staging a dynamic spectacle of a "metropolitan subject," the new city part removes itself from the danger of uniformity on a grand scale.

This becomes an adventure played on the edges, on the borders between juxtaposed spatial entities, lively fringes that separate the built-up sections, in an alternation between vehicle flow and pedestrianism. Euralille builds its own urban identity precisely on the "fringes" – on the spaces in between – rather than on the "monuments" that it erects. Increasing the value of the residual dimension generated by the collage-like approach of Koolhaas, the Parc Matisse of Gilles Clément is the most important of these interspaces. If OMA envisaged an artificial space of Alphandian origin for the park, subject to a transformation into an infrastructure and mineral spectacle, Clément's proposal proceeds instead from the recognition and celebration of the intrinsic values of a *terrain vague*. And it is capable of suspending, if only momentarily, the condition of eradication and standardization, a result of the new city. Clément distances himself from neo-illuminist illusion of being able to manipulate the world unconditionally and criticizes the transformative enthusiasm fed by the Euralille operation. As a work of refitting and maintenance, the idealized rebuilding of a piece of prime and "inviolate" European forest gets placed on the pedestal of the Ile Derborence. In the Bois des Transparences, along shady routes, *jardins planétaires, jardins en mouvement, pyro-paysages*, recreated little by little, allow the glass volumes and the changing surfaces of the "business city" to be glimpsed as they emerge among the tree branches like ready-made landscapes. A diachronic reading of the land and the recovery of the time frame in Clément's garden – *à réaction poétique* – succeeds in creating a contrast between the modernity of the buildings in the background and the wild nature in which one is immersed. This is the illusion of recreating here and now an Olympian balance of a Le Corbusier-type matrix that surrenders sleepily to the dynamism of Koolhaas "immersed in the air and light."

From the park, across the arcades of the Le Corbusier Viaduct, one accesses the segmented triangle, conjoining the geometries of the development and that symbol of the impact between buildings and infrastructures that is Mitterrand Square. What inspires interest in this irregular interspace, more than the form of the objects that circumscribe it, is the character of what is left and the accumulation of the various urban visions created. It represents an interactive and functional space for the coexistence of "urban actors," each of whom is reserved a personal scenario. The main locations are the groupings of tracks of the existing station of Lille Flandres, aligned with the *centre commercial* Euralille of Nouvel, and the new TGV Lille Europe Station of Duthilleul, towered over by the Vasconi and Porzamparc skyscrapers.

Far from the exuberant monumentalism of the train stations planned in the same years by the SNCF, the Lille Europe Station is a simple sequence of galleries, covered by a light roofing by Rice, that from Mitterrand Square rises to the Boulevard de Turin. From here one catches sight of the incremental undertakings of the "second phase" of Euralille, which densify the fringes between the various infrastructures and the station: Delhay's Cité des affaires, Mateo's Cité de l'Europe, and De Geyter's St Maurice neighbourhood on Valladolid Square. A wooden pier suspended over the highway, the square accommodates routes from the new developments on the margins of the conurbation. And it is the open-air atrium from which one accesses the "Piranesi-like space," an extruded cube forty metres in depth that transports the travellers coming from the Meteor to the different levels, parking lots, the station, or the city. An urban decompression chamber sorts the flow of traffic and human movements, and again presents, in this version of an excavated foot-print, the themes of the hybrid and overcrowded cube already tested by OMA in the projects of the ZKM in Karlsruhe and at the Très Grande Bibliothèque in Paris.

In 1997, after the deviation of the Boulevard périphérique est through to the Parc des Dondaines, the express route was transformed by OMA into an urban boulevard flanking the Grand Palais and thus connected to the city. A tripartite hybrid receptacle along the axis of the ellipse, it expresses the dissymmetry between the urban side and the side facing the infrastructures. The brutalist use of "poor" and seemingly not durable materials is a return to designs of stadiums and fair pavilions, for example, and abandons the ambition to evoke the *firmitas* of a civic monument. The wavy and shifting wall allows one to glimpse the enlargements of Euralille 2000–10 from the urban boulevard.

Following an incremental approach, construction continues along the free margins between OMA's development and the surrounding city, making use of previous successes. Dislocated volumes densify the Grand Boulevard junction in the Romarin neighbourhood, while the infill of properties carved out of the St Maurice neighbourhood highlights the infrastructure geometry. The "*bois habité*" and the new headquarters of the Region Nord-Pas de Calais will form the end of the southern fringe. The success of these undertakings depends on the previous ones, which transformed a problematic *terrain vague* into a lively part of the city, and amid infinite contradictions and results, differing from expectations, brought about lasting results.

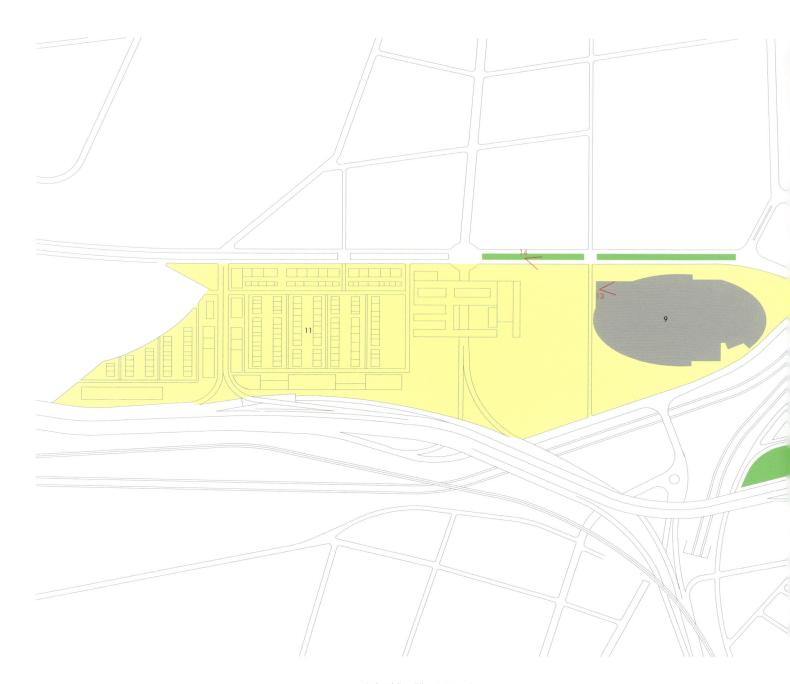

**Lille**, Euralille

Urban planning and coordination: OMA
Development company: Seam Euralille
Planning and implementation: 1991–2009

1 Ccial Euralille: J. Nouvel
2 WTC: C. Vasconi
3 Credit Lyonnais: C. De Portzamparc
4 Gare Lille Europe: J.M. Duthilleul, P. Rice
5 Viaduct Le Corbusier: F. Deslaugiers
6 Parc Matisse: G. Clément, Empreinte
7 Crown Plaza: M. e F. Delhay
8 Axe Europe: L. Mateo, F. Andrieux
9 Lille Grand Palais: OMA
10 Saint-Maurice: X. De Geyter, Laloux & Lebecq, F. Fendrich (urban plan)
11 Euralille 2–Bois Habité: F. Leclercq, M. Guthmann, TER (urban plan)

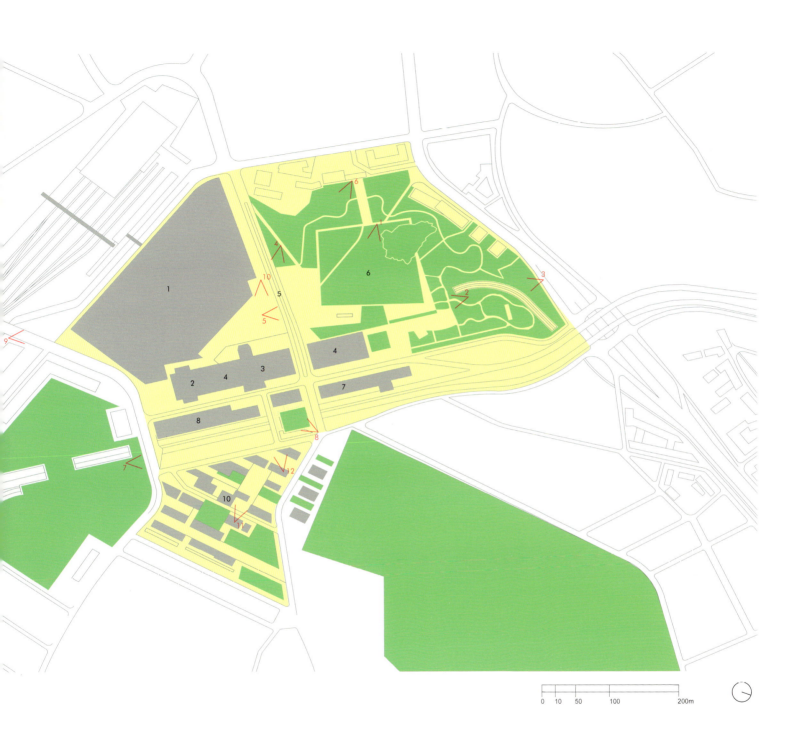

# **Lisbon**, Expo98, Gare do Oriente, Parque do Tejo

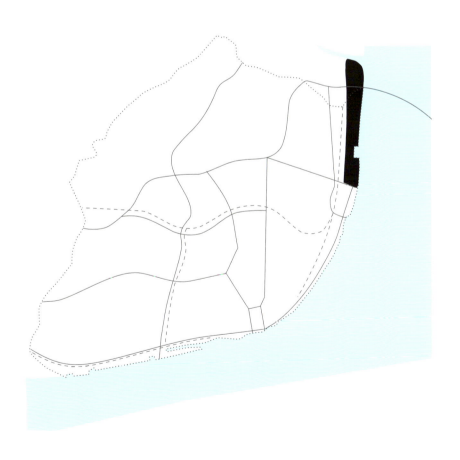

The completion of Expo '98, "Seas and Oceans," is the crowning achievement of the 1994 nomination of Lisbon as the European capital of culture and of Portugal's entry into the European Community. A new dynamic of public and private investment in Lisbon was translated into projects of great urban scope, including the recovery of abandoned industrial areas, the construction of new road infrastructures, the modernizing of the existing railway network, the defining of large leisure and entertainment areas on a metropolitan scale, the rethinking of the relationship between the city and the Tagus River, a frontage of nearly twenty kilometres.

Launched in 1992, the Lisbon strategic plan interrupts the passivity of the 1980s and implements an amalgam of sectoral plans that, together with restoration programs for the existing city, open up unexpected perspectives of renewal and modernization for the entire metropolitan conurbation. In particular, the Project for the Expansion of the Metro, the Plans for the Organization of the Harbour Area and the Metropolitan Area, the Expo '98 project, and the plans for infrastructure reform with new road and rail bridges over the Tagus River have permitted the channelling of national and international and private and public investments in a poly-articular but cohesive urban and landscape strategy, thus ushering in previously unknown opportunities for Lisbon.

With the Expo '98 came the opportunity to launch a thorough reconversion of the harbour and industrial area to the east of the city, one of the most deteriorated and devastated sectors of Lisbon. Even though locating the structure of Expo '98 in such an area brought with it huge financial and technical resources, which bound the city for over eight years, the greatest burden lay with the urban restructuring plan of an industrial area five kilometres long. It was necessary to proceed with an environmental cleanup, and with the Exhibition Park (Parque das Nações), the provision of large urban facilities was required. To foster the integration of the historic city with the existing conurbation, new transit infrastructures were built, and the metropolitan and railway line was extended to merge in the interchange station of the Gare do Oriente. On the other hand, the structures connected with Expo were not designed exclusively for the transitory nature of the event; rather, they were meant to be lasting connective elements in the urban physiology: so it is with the Oceanarium, the Sports Pavilion, the Portugal Pavilion, the Pavilions of the Participating Nations salvaged for fair functions, the multi-use Atlantic Pavilion, now re-used as the Convention Centre, the Garcia de Orta Gardens, and the Parque do Tejo and Trancão.

We find the Gare do Oriente, Portugal's principal intermodal station, finally attaining a view on the Tagus, right in the centre of this large urban and landscape renewal. Because of the exceptionality of the event and the emergency situation thus created, public institutions and municipal corporations had to overcome sectoral separations, divisions of expertise, and mutual mistrust: only an expanded dialogue, a convergence of objectives, and a profitable cooperation allowed the urban infrastructure under construction to interchange with different transit modes. For the first time in Portugal, subways, trains, and buses reach the centre of the metropolitan conurbation of Lisbon in a unified solution.

In 1994, Santiago Calatrava won the competition for the Gare do Oriente with a plan that Barata, citing the Viennese art historian Riegl, defines as an "intentional monument": a monument to the contemporary, near the centre of Lisbon so that the "need for a modern iconography would not be limited to new urban agglomerates, but would also concern the historic centre of the European city, already packed with monuments and ancient buildings of all types." With the right impetus, Calatrava goes beyond the idea of the station as "civic architecture," an idea that still informs Moneo Staion in Madrid or Cruz y Ortiz in Seville. Having abandoned the energetic rhetoric that four years earlier had given shape to the TGV Station of Lyon-Satolas, he rediscovers here a sort of dematerialized monumentality – light. As if it were a large greenhouse or a bower in the park, it exalts the station building dissolving it in the constituent infrastructure elements: bridges, bus shelters, boardwalks, canopies, ramps. If the plan's approach seems similar to Zurich's Stadelhofen, in the Gare do Oriente it is an exquisitely urban goal that gives new meaning to a difficult concentration of complex organisms in a highly reactive context, whereas, in the Stadelhofen, the landscape dimension predominates as it reaches the city via the infrastructure.

Calatrava carefully opens out the city at the back of the railroad towards the Tagus, with the bridge deck of the tracks – one hundred metres wide – supported by a succession of five flexible concrete segmented arch bridges. A gigantic lift table caught in the act of raising a slab of earth, doubling its urban functionality, is an idealized representation of effort in motion. *Earthwork*, Frampton would call it, is an immense enclosure that accommodates public services, and descends to the subway and the bus shelters. Above, there is a "garden" of metallic palms towering over the podium, a strange surrealist landscape that sorts the rail travellers as a substitute for a "station building" that no longer has a raison d'être.

Born around the time of the exhibition, Gare do Oriente is the symbolic access gate to the city. The arcades give a glimpse of the Doca, the old wet dock of the naval shipyards that Manuel Salgado, designer of the open spaces of the Parque das Nações, symbolically and figuratively locates at the centre of the exhibition enclosure. As in the foundation city, orthogonal routes circumscribe the city blocks, carve out urban public spaces, and accommodate the routes coming from the neighbourhoods to the north, absorbing the fluvial marshes and the infrastructure imprint of the wet dock, which the Portuguese Pavilion of Alvaro Siza overlooks, as well as the Oceanarium of Peter Chermayeff, the Knowledge of the Seas Pavilion of Carrilho da Graça, and the Multi-purpose Pavilion of Cruz and SOM.

The strength of the urban plan lies in having provided strategic value to the ground design, understood as the integrated interweaving between the formation of the open spaces and the infrastructure plan. The Calçada in white stone is the large structure that possesses enough autonomy and technical complexity to be able to thoroughly absorb the disparate underground technological components and the network of underground services. A large public space that identifies the banks of the Tagus, the squares between buildings, the walkways along the parks and gardens, the Calçada is also the element that provides resistance to the urban form in the metamorphosis from the Expo enclosure to the actual city section.

To the northeast, the urban grid becomes distorted and unravels before the land infrastructure reality, losing itself in the orographic fade-out of the broad landscape of the Parque do Tejo and do Trancão into the confluence of the rivers of the same name. These landscapes provide complex ecological cleanup and water and air purification mechanisms while functioning and being enjoyed as a metropolitan park. This large urban infrastructure, extending over ninety hectares, offers sports and leisure activities, phyto-purification, and garbage recycling facilities, and incorporates the highway junctions connecting to Ponte Vasco da Gama Bridge, built concurrently with Expo98. Playing fields, tennis courts, equestrian areas, and amphitheatres for shows and festivals coexist with the Lisbon's largest water purification system, where the waters are collected, filtered, and then introduced into the Tagus. On the inside, an environmental research centre monitors the reclamation activities, operating like an interface between work, research, and education, with the task of educating visitors and illustrating the environmental and ecological problems.

In the reclamation of the swamps, planners George Hargreaves and João Nunes shape three metres of artificial soil, furrowing the topographical plate of the site inserted beneath the river height, in a succession of ridges and valleys. The plastic manipulation digs the sediments from the drainage and brings them back to the surface to form dunes and verges, and if, in one respect, this refers to the slow action of wind and water on the millennial corrosion that has moulded the river estuary, on the other, it triggers the lengthy transformation process of orographic modelling. With an alternation of processes of deviation, regulation, and channelling of the waters, the mass of sedimentary detritus transported by the currents is pushed forward to be deposited in specific strategic points. Skilfully controlled, the natural process of river water sedimentation implements environmental regeneration, and absorbs mobility and technical systems, in an ever-changing tangle of fractal geometry to provide the park with a sense of unity and figurative content on a grand scale – on the land scale of the lengthy viaduct, to which it forms a contrast, and which gets reabsorbed into the spectacle of a monumental landscape.

**Lisbon**, Expo98, Gare do Oriente, Parque do Tejo

Urban plan of the Parque das Nações: Vassalo Rosa, Manuel Salgado
Architectural plan of the Gare do Oriente: Santiago Calatrava
Plan of the Parque do Tejo e do Trancão: George Hargreaves, João Nunes
Development company: Parque Expo
Planning and implementation: 1993–1998

1 Gare do Oriente: S. Calatrava
2 Pavilion of Portugal: A. Siza
3 Oceanarium: P. Chermayeff
4 Atlantic Pavillion: R. Cruz, SOM
5 Knowledge of the Seas Pavilion: C. da Graça
6 FIL Feira Internacional de Lisboa
7 Garcia de Orta gardens: J. Gomes da Silva
8 Vasco da Gama tower: L. Janeiro, SOM
9 Parque do Tejo e do Trancão: G. Hargreaves, J. Nunes
10 Vasco da Gama Bridge

# London, Canary Wharf

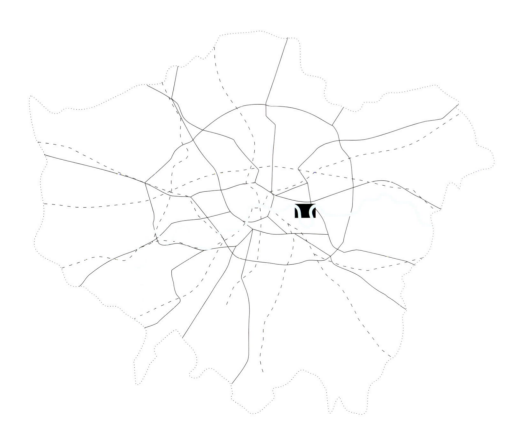

Since the 1980s, Great Britain, in distancing itself from the general European orientation on the question of urban policies, has noticeably directed its approaches to urban transformation towards the private investment market. Having set aside the lengthy tradition of comprehensive planning, and guided by North American practices and policies, Great Britain began to formulate methods of engaging private enterprise. A different operating scenario into urban renewal was thus initiated, while the rest of Europe continued, until the mid 1990s, to conduct such operations mostly on the basis of public capital initiatives.

Elected prime minister at the end of the 1970s, Margaret Thatcher enacted a liberalist policy, similar to Ronald Reagan's in the United States, that outlined three planned undertakings – privatization, deregulation, marketization – which were then transferred to the areas of construction and urban renewal. Thatcherism was committed to dissolving the link between urban planning and the welfare state, which, for a long time, symbolized the administrative tradition of Labour governments. This shift had major repercussions on the urban reform and construction processes at a time when recession had already triggered a phase of de-industrialization and industry closures. The relocation of production left brownfield sites in the urban centres of Manchester, Liverpool, and Birmingham. The evolution of commercial maritime transport towards containers and offshore interchange platforms, which initiated one of the worst urban and social crises of the last century, reduced London harbour activities and ultimately brought closures that left kilometres of docks in disuse. Contrary to what was proposed and carried out by the public policies of the 1950s and 1960s, the government handled the emergency by providing incentives and involving "free enterprise" in large-scale urban transformation investments that were meant to create employment and facilitate the physical regeneration of the areas. Public interference was meant to be limited in order to promote leverage phenomena, and to attract and, at the same time, optimize private capital investments with multiplier effects.

Established in 1980, the urban development corporations (UDC), one of the most important initiatives of the Thatcher government, grafts principles of American-style leverage planning onto previous practices of public building development, widely tested by the New Town Development Corporation in the construction of a new town. As with the New York State Development Corporation of 1968, public capital is not invested. With the role of developer abandoned, only the implementation of real estate development operations in critical urban sectors is reserved for the promoter, thus activating the process of improving the value of these areas in different ways. A land use plan is drafted to identify new functions and work out infrastructure projects aimed at optimizing and increasing accessibility. It launches operations of urban marketing for opening onto the free market, and it triggers policies of tax exemption to attract financial capital.

At the beginning of the 1980s, the main industrial cities of the United Kingdom were already considering the setting up of thirteen of these corporations, one of which is the London Docklands Development Corporation, which brought about the renewal of London's Docklands. In this case, an additional and fundamental means for attracting investments and creating real estate development opportunities was the Enterprise Zone (EZ). Established for the first time in 1982 for Canary Wharf at the Isle of Dogs in the Docklands, the EZ has a complex and still debated origin. Derived in part from the American Urban Development Grant of 1977, it was anticipated by the intuitions of Pnoeter Hall when, in 1975, he coined the definition of the non-plan-area, taking as reference the deregulation executed by Hong Kong and the "Asian Tigers."

In the setting up of an EZ one relies on the arrangement of "flexible" strategies "guided by demand," rather than by management criteria offered by morphological and conceptual policies.

Indeed, Canary Wharf, and other later Enterprise Zones, totally lack planning and morphological guidance: the same developers worked out the plan, introducing a functional mix and an investment plan. Criticized for having damaged the democratic principles of decision-making procedures, the Canary Wharf project, which is predicted to have over a million square metres of surface, twenty-four office blocks, and three 250-metre towers, was nonetheless approved within two weeks after a "fast-track" process.

As opposed to other less contested EZs that involved re-use and recovery of existing industrial building structures, what has aroused confusion and worried the public and architects here is the new design and build, which would not only completely transform the Isle of Dogs but supplant, like a symbolic and settlement alternative, nothing less than the "square mile" of the City. The urban image proposed by SOM for the Canadian Olympia & York more than anything else generated reservations and apprehension: the Beaux Arts legacy, reaching America through the "Great Good City" by Daniel Burnham, returned to Europe a year later as an exercise in urban thematics. This represents a gigantic simulation of urban character, well-known and stereotyped for being ready to be inserted into the recreation market. Often similarities and influences are traced back to European models such as the Défense. But, from an urban-financial standpoint, this theme park points mostly towards the festival marketplaces of James Rouse, in which a mix of attractions and entertainment is blended with shopping centres, offices, and themed residences, all defined by the environmental qualities of the landscape and the water.

For Baltimore's waterfront, Rouse, in fact, executes Disneyland-type strategies to attract millions of visitors and customers. This represents the common reference model of waterfront regeneration promoted during the 1980s and 1990s in the largest North American ports – Boston, Miami, and New York – for which the Canadian Olympia & York was actually one of the principal developers. The entertainment themes of the festival marketplaces, on the other hand, in a conveniently moderate way resort to the redevelopments of the 1990s of other European port cities like Barcelona, Genoa, Rotterdam, Oslo, and Hamburg.

Despite controversial and fluctuating circumstances during the implementation phase, such as the change in ownership after the recession crisis at the end of the 1980s, it can be said that Canary Wharf, having obtained with the Limehouse Link tunnel and the Jubilee Line Extension an adequate and fast connection with the city, now represents one of the most attractive and vital parts of London. It is necessary to recognize that, within the context of the global competition between New York, Tokyo, Frankfurt, and Singapore, the Canary Wharf district has allowed London to reaffirm itself among the most important international centres of the financial market, thus winning the banking race.

An urban block design tries to reproduce a dense city: it arranges city blocks along the existing port basins that, being absorbed into the morphology of the whole, lend specific environmental values to the site. Urban spaces in the Beaux Arts tradition, simplified and adapted to the use of the automobile during the American decline of the 1920s, structure the central mall above the shopping gallery and the parking lots. Arcades, staircases, and flower beds increase public enjoyment even in the lobbies of the hotels and management offices. The headquarters' tower for the HSBC of Foster & Partners and the one for the Upper Bank by KPF flank the previous landmark of C. Pelli on Canada Place. Rising from the central parterre following a hybrid model, a tower block, which evokes the congested skyline of an American downtown, is erected like a local landmark and is visible from the distance. Such a soaring of towers, defended by their symbolic and representative aspirations, initially unleashed complaints and protests for the excessive "Americanization" that it transmitted, since the proposed building density was not much more than that of Georgian Bloomsbury. Squares, parks and gardens, treed boulevards, atriums of buildings, shopping arcades, parking, and the great halls of the train and metro stations are laced into the continuity of a pedestrian space, fully accessible and barely disturbed by vehicle traffic, but reserved for taxis, public buses, and service facilities. One can definitely state that SOM, in the creation of the morphological layout, began with conceiving the open spaces: right from the beginning the landscapers from the studio of Hanna & Olin were involved in the planning. Once the "profitable part" of the project was specified, it was important to establish the "character" of the whole and study in depth the urban spaces and the building facades.

The project competitions and the consultations, in which, among others, KPF, Koetter & Kim, Rossi, and McAlsan participated, were reserved solely for the planning of the facades, since the volumetric forms, the ground-structure interaction, the gates, entrance halls, and internal distribution of the buildings had already been precisely defined by SOM.

In the 1980s, the first operating phase builds on the Thames River bays, around Westferry Circus and Cabot Square. The buildings planned by SOM, KPF, Koetter & Kim, and Pei Cobb Freed, reproducing and simulating an imaginary American metropolis present in historicist architecture, hint at the art deco New York of the 1930s and echo the Chicago School.

Facing out onto the Greenwich peninsula and around Canada Place and at Jubilee Park, the buildings of the second phase, designed by C. Pelli, Foster & Partners, SOM, KPF, and HOK, comfortably followed the trend of technological architecture: sleekness and grace expressed in the large glassed-in halls, translucent stone slabs, metallic grills, reflecting sheets of steel and bronze, and structural windows. Even the compelling conception of the open spaces, oriented towards the recovery of "urban conventions" such as circuses, squares, boulevards, and avenues, weakens, which leaves the gardens and landscaping, Jubilee Park, and the glass "bubbles" from the Jubilee Line more freely integrated among the architectures, infrastructures, open spaces, and environment. The transformative pressure that Canary Wharf places on the interior is substantial. And it succeeds in triggering renovation processes on derelict parts of the city, pushing for the recovery of deteriorated buildings and warehouses that face out onto the adjacent river basins, while other recent interventions around it, with offices, housing, and commercial activities together, are attempting to spoil the initial mono-functional defect and lessen its original fate, in order to make it more fully functional.

**London**, Canary Wharf

Urban planning and coordination: SOM
Development company: Canary Wharf Group Plc
Planning and implementation: 1986–ongoing

1. Westferry Circus: Hanna & Olin
2. 1, 2, 11 Westferry Circus: SOM, Koetter & Kim, Perkins & Will
3. 15 Westferry Circus: Farrell & Partners
4. 17 Columbus Courtyard: Gensler & Associates
5. 20 Columbus Courtyard: SOM
6. Credit Suisse: Pei Coob Freed & Partners
7. 25 Cabot Square: SOM
8. 20 Cabot Square: KPF
9. 10 Cabot Square: SOM
10. Cabot Square: Hanna & Olin
11. Docklands Light Railway Station
12. 25 North Colonnade: T. McAslan, Adamson Associates
13. 30 South Colonnade: KPF
14. One Canada Square: Pelli & Associates
15. 5 Canada Square: SOM
16. 8 Canada Square: Foster & Partners
17. 33 Canada Square: Foster & Partners
18. 25 Canada Square: Pelli & Associates
19. Canada Square Park: Hanna & Olin
20. 15 Canada Square: KPF
21. Canada Place: C. Taylor
22. 20 Canada Square: SOM
23. One Churchill Place: HOK
24. 20 Bank Street: SOM
25. 25 Bank Street: Pelli & Associates
26. West Wintergarden: Pelli & Associates
27. 40 Bank Street: Pelli & Associates
28. East Wintergarden: Pelli & Associates
29. 50 Bank Street: Pelli & Associates
30. 10 Upper Bank Street: KPF
31. Jubilee Park: P. Wirtz
32. 25 Churchill Place: KPF
33. 20 Churchill Place: KPF
34. 5 Churchill Place: HOK

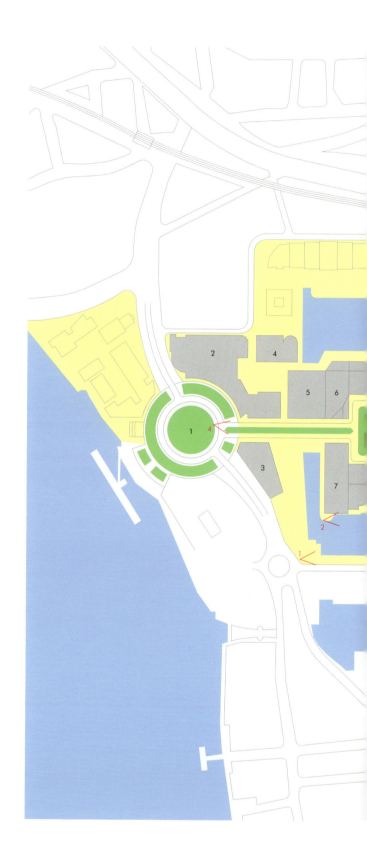

# **Milan**, Grande Bicocca

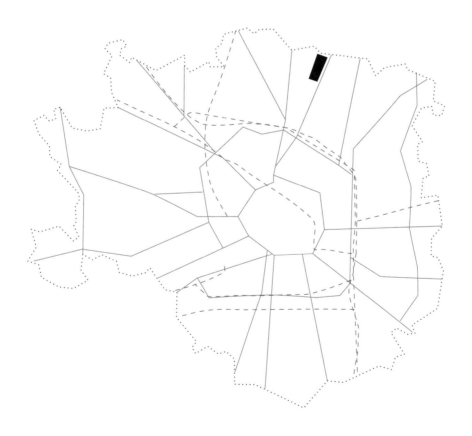

Grande Bicocca enters into urban Milanese history at the beginning of the 1980s, navigating its way through policies and urban reorganization that were painstakingly taking shape at the time. In Europe during these years, the idea of "special projects" was hovering in the air as an alternative to urban planning. Discussion on this subject begins in Milan with the *Documento Direttore del Progetto Passante* (The general document for the Interchange Link Project) of 1984. Attempting to respond to the urban crisis of the 1970s, which was the result of industry closures, large projects connected to the reorganization of the metropolitan infrastructure system were undertaken. The interchange railway link was to enhance the northwest–southeast axis, a historic axis that structured the city's relationship to the surrounding territory, via the underground connection of Bovisa Station with the Garibaldi, Vittoria, and Rogoredo stations. The new urban and territorial accessibility would promote the localization of "important functions" in the brownfield sites along the route. In fact, the lack of reliability of the implementation procedures of the *Documento Direttore*, the "area projects," and the slowness in the execution of the interchange link prevented the projects' achievement as well as the start of a great many of the proposed changes.

During this stalemate, the Technology Centre project was put forward. The centre was to be built on the abandoned Bicocca sites of Pirelli Spa. It was ratified in the 1985 protocol agreement and promoted through an international architecture competition won by the firm of Gregotti Associati in 1987. From a strategic point of view, it is clear how a large transformation project in the Bicocca area would be in opposition to the urban policies that were being outlined with such difficulty. If it was legitimate and necessary to pose the question of the "urban sprawl of the Milanese northeast," and to have envisaged in the Bicocca area the virtual centre of gravity of such a conurbation, it is now necessary to acknowledge, with the project almost completed, that a strategy on an overall urban scale has been missing, something that in Barcelona, for example, "returns the city to the sea," or in Paris rehabilitated the east, or in Amsterdam reconnects the port to the city. In Milan, which from the 1980s saw a constant fragmentation in the transformation processes, even the Bicocca project acquired aspects of an Enterprise Zone, which Pirelli Spa was firmly intending to bring about.

This is a circumstance that imposed limits to the urban planning, which was forced to operate within an enclave of property boundaries, and was unable to engage in a broad-spectrum shared urban strategy. The idea of going beyond the enclosure in order to physically enter the surrounding city was hypothesized by Gregotti, Rossi, and Valle in their respective competition designs, which showed that the project would have had to act on an "intermediary scale" between the new development and the city, and reach levels of complexity capable of interconnecting the different urban systems, including housing, infrastructure, and public transit.

In an effort to form a "historic centre on the outskirts" – in other words, to structure a new centre and a reference point for the conurbation north of Milan – the Bicocca project established a structured layout where a chaotic territorial spread of the settlements mixes with the remnants of a changing industrial periphery. In conceiving morphological characteristics, an option for a regular city is unveiled – one that is orderly and organically interrelated so as to be recognizable within the urban sprawl. Five superblocks are defined in different morphologies and are subjected to a symmetrical axis, thus constituting the "central spine" – a general principle that organizes the structure: it determines the articulations between spaces and buildings, it joins up with the perimeter of the development unit, and, by reclaiming the configuration of the existing streets and the scale of the abandoned industrial buildings, it organizes a new hierarchy of internal relations and of relations with the city. A fully equipped axis route interacts with three systems that are constructed perpendicular to it.

To the north, a "bastion" with parking and gardens crosses through the existing sports centre to end in the residential island that rises up into a bipartite housing block. In the centre, the Esplanade along Sarca Boulevard is centred symmetrically onto La Piazza (The Square), a low-slung shopping centre surrounded by residential towers. To the south, the axis of symmetry of Emanueli Street reunites the science departments of the university, the residential courtyards, and the Greco train station. In the "resulting spaces" between the city and the prioritized places, we have the triangle of the Teatro degli Arcimboldi (Arcimboldi Theatre), the Collina dei Ciliegi (Cherry Hill), and the offices of the Pirelli group.

Like the University of Calabria, which was planned in the 1970s by the Gregotti group and includes a light pedestrian bridge that reunites individual objects to formulate a structured layout on a territorial scale, so, too, in the Bicocca area, a virtual axis of symmetry adds on, one after the other, the superblocks of the central spine for over a kilometre. Keeping five entities unified by having to give up a real continuity of build caused Gregotti to execute a careful strategy of deployment, organized in compositional hierarchies and substantiated by morphological and architectural cross-references: bilateral symmetry, surface and volumetric structuring, reiteration of architectural and linguistic sets of rules, which only one single and very determined planner would have been able to contain in an organic whole. The Gregotti Associati firm, a unifying planning body, builds from time to time, and from product to product, the conditions of a relational logic between the parts, on the inside of the virtual surface/volumetric context and of the real context, as determined by successive additions.

The coordinator-architect even takes on the role of designer of every object and all the open spaces – a "self-coordination," therefore, that has the responsibility of actualizing the surface/volumetric composition and the preliminary plans, tempering, during the operational process, the fragmenting of times and spaces generated by the dynamic management of the operation. Not even the practical alterations or the intervening changes of use – from "Techno-city" in the 1980s through the "historic centre of the outskirts" in the 1990s and culminating in the "Grande Bicocca" in 2000 – could cut into the organic structure of the whole, so strong was the determination to build according to fixed surface/volumetric rules. The firmness with which Gregotti pursues this unified image seems to be an answer as well as a precaution with respect to such a feverish management style: he feared that he could lose the control over the quality of the development. In similar circumstances, in which the fragmented nature of management is accompanied by a radical change in goals, outcomes, and functions along the way, it is necessary to recognize also that the pact of solidarity between planner and client has been an indispensible guarantee of morphological control.

With essentially architectural and compositional measures, different levels of relationships between the parts and the whole are established. Applied on an urban scale, a kind of Durand-style combination theory is implemented in forms drawn from the anthology of Gregotti's architectural passions: the organicism of Oud and Dudok, the rationalism of Libera and Terragni, the moderate classicism of Berhens and Poelzig. A *dispositio* (layout), executed in different interacting steps, is based on the rearrangement of spaces and times, by keeping the fixed part within the planimetric/volumetric composition. On the "city scale," one resorts to the counterpoint of emergent structures: landmarks that stand out in their singularity of character and at the same time relate to each other by a recurrence of architectural systems. On the "intermediary urban scale," a gigantic layout of building arrangements and bow windows is presented to give shape to the open spaces. On the "construction level," regular sequences of window openings, grill arrangements, modulated panellings, and repeated architectural elements reinforce a principle of homologation, identifying the development in terms of its internal homogeneity. Narrow passages, gates, and cutouts into the volumes make the axes of symmetry visible as well, while a deployment strategy of colours and recurring materials identifies related complexes.

The desire to pursue organicity and continuity promotes osmosis between pre-existing industrial architecture and new architecture. The regularity of the previous factories on a grand scale is again suggested in the modular configurations of the new, just as the styles adopted for the new compositional elements are transferred, in turn, onto the buildings to be renovated, thus becoming standardized and assimilated to the whole. Perret undertakes revitalization towards the same end when, in Le Havre, he seeks a balance between building variety and the organicity of the whole in a style substantiated by technical and structural realities and by a system of modulation that supports the assembly of standardized elements. On the Bicocca project, the standardization on a grand scale of an industrial world is repeatedly evoked by the facade details. By evocation we mean: surface cladding, skins, coatings, and ventilated walls, which reproduce perceptual effects that refer to industrial building systems where traditional construction methods linger.

Gregotti interprets the city block as a module of an organic and unified structure of macrostructural origin, and the planning takes shape starting from the "full extent" of the newly built. In the shape of the city block, relatively independent structures find their own raison d'être within their perimeters. They establish mostly connecting and access relations with the street, internally reabsorbing the urban dynamism. The streets are only the start of the perimeter and the functional connection with the development entities, while the urban spaces are mere "voids," the result of the juxtaposition of the building volumes.

In 2009, the development agency Pirelli RE decided to expand the settlement towards the north, absorbing the Ex Ansaldo areas. By anchoring itself to the arrangement of the large axialities of Bicocca and Ansaldo, the urban and landscape design of the Grande Bicocca, formulated by Giuseppe Marinoni, introduces elements of continuity as well as strong discontinuity with the existing neighbourhood. Above all, the new plan gives fundamental value to the open space, and no longer, and only, to the buildings. Such a field shift sets out to produce a relatively unified layout in the utilization and perception of the configured urban spaces. Four large gardens enter into a synergistic relationship, in terms of structure and function, with the existing urban spaces. New paths shape the gardens and, at the same time, have the value of foundation lines in the outlining of the positioning of new buildings, strategically located to communicate with the existing neighbourhood and to define the open spaces that have been generated.

**Milan**, Grande Bicocca

Urban planning and coordination: Gregotti Associati
Landscape plan: Andreas Kipar-Land
Urban and landscape planning "Nuovo Centro Grande Bicocca": StudioMarinoni
Development company: Pirelli RE
Planning and implementation: 1987–ongoing

1 Deutsche Bank: G. Valle
2 Offices: Gregotti Associati
3 Gruppo Siemens: Gregotti Associati
4 Dipartimenti scientifici Università degli Studi di Milano: Gregotti Associati
5 Sede del Consiglio Nazionale delle Ricerche: Gregotti Associati
6 Cooperative: Gregotti Associati
7 Collina dei Ciliegi: A. Kipar-Land
8 Residence Esplanade: Gregotti Associati
9 Residence Le torri: Gregotti Associati
10 Teatro Arcimboldi: Gregotti Associati
11 Cooperative: Gregotti Associati
12 Università degli Studi di Milano: Gregotti Associati
13 Pirelli Headquarters: Gregotti Associati
14 Centro Ricerca Pneumatici Pirelli: Gregotti Associati
15 Centro Ricerca Cavi Pirelli: Boeri Studio
16 Bicocca Village: B. Camerana
17 Hangar Bicocca: Cerri & Colombo Associati
18 'Nuovo Centro Grande Bicocca': StudioMarinoni

7
8

11
12

# **Milan**, Nuova Portello

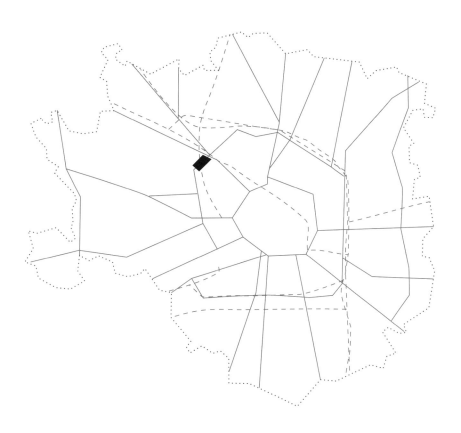

The general document for the Interchange Link Project of 1984 inaugurates the era of "special projects" in Milan as an alternative to the comprehensive planning of the regulatory plan in force, the cause of procedural inactivity and lack of effectiveness in generating a high construction quality in the transformation processes. Such a document is one of the first attempts, both analytical and exploratory, to weigh the effects of the abandoned areas and seize the land resource as an opportunity, which, between brownfield sites and railway yards, counts for more than a quarter of the municipal area. The abandoned sites of the gas storage tanks in the Bovisa neighbourhood, the former Alfa Romeo plant in the Portello neighbourhood, the Montedison group in the Rogoredo neighbourhood, the Garibaldi Repubblica area – all united at the Farini, Vittoria, and Romana yards – become, in the Interchange Link Project, potential new centres, parts of a complex urban plan of infrastructure and urban reorganization that has its greatest strength in the rail link, enhancing the historic northwest–southeast axis via the underground connection of the Bovisa Station with the Garibaldi, Vittoria, and Rogoredo stations.

Among these "special projects," Nuova Portello, on the disused former Alfa Romeo and former Lancia sites, is the one that has most contributed to generate a high-quality urban and settlement life, launching a renewal process of the northeast section of the city of Milan, including the reorganization of the urban exhibition and convention centre and, subsequently, the renewal of the former exhibition complex with the CityLife project. The access gateway to the city from the north highway system, Nuova Portello is located over the ring road of Serra Boulevard, on the stretch bordered by the two north–west routes that link the centre of the city to the highways.

In 2001, the municipality and the Nuova Portello and Auredia associations drew up the plan agreement to launch the integrated program of rehabilitation works with the goal of constructing a city section that, in integrating itself into the surrounding urban fabric, could give shape to the empty space left over from the demolition of the industrial premises. The functional mix is common to most other neighbourhoods starting up in the semi-central areas of Milan at the time, which include housing, a shopping mall, parking areas, offices, and half of the land surface intended as a park.

If the high-quality results of Nuova Portello differ enormously from the other neighbourhoods built in those years in Milan, almost all rather disappointing, this is solely due to the quality of the urban and architectural plan of Gino Valle and the management of the enlightened clientele guided by Ennio Brion.

The urban plan is formulated here as a planimetric/volumetric one that establishes the layout of the build and the configuration of the open spaces. As a result, the planners are asked to develop an architectural plan based precisely on the urban principles outlined by Valle.

Valle stages a kind of collage between cities made up of blocks and buildings arranged *en plein air*. It represents the will and desire to rebuild the form of the existing city centred on the trident generated by Accursio Square, and to respond, at the same time, to the infrastructure impetus of Scarampo Boulevard coming from the highway and Serra Boulevard that cuts the area in two. The desire to make two urban models collide is understood in the choice of the size of the city blocks that define the borders of Traiano Street – a curtain-like building structure to define the street front and an open building structure with towers and blocks, thought to be more suited to articulate the view on the park.

Even the shopping mall in this design is broken up in order to be reorganized as an ensemble of city blocks of different sizes and gathered together in a cluster – a kind of citadel where commercial buildings, open spaces, and underground parking lots are integrated together to express an urban dimension that also succeeds in removing itself from the limitations of the thematic framework. As an economic engine of a real estate development operation, the shopping centre also becomes the morphological engine of the entire complex here, solely due to the conceptual and management farsightedness of planner and client. It is, in fact, from the open spaces of the commercial centre that the long lines of the routes depart and generate the open spaces and the positioning of the buildings.

This shopping centre as conceived by Valle is composed of five blocks — a kind of typological collage between the large-scale commercial areas and the "fabric" of the stores. A deployment strategy based on a morphology of interacting levels creates "streets" and "squares," blending the shopping centre model with the outlet model. With this example, we are approaching, for the first time in Italy, the European examples of the urban commercial district, represented in this book by the Stadshart of Almere — a model that, in distancing itself from the mono-functional container of the mega-structure type, attempts to generate morphological and functional variety that echoes the "natural shopping centre," such as one finds in several European and Italian urban centres.

A canopy fifteen metres high identifies the "cover" of the main square and becomes the symbolic and functional fulcrum of the open-space system. From here, the arrival of stairs and escalators connects the urban level to the underground level of parking lots and exhibition and service zones.

The entire zone is pedestrianized. Valle strategically positions the automobile and service accesses in more than one point, masterfully joining them up with the street system of the surrounding city without introducing suburban traffic morphologies, as often occurs in these types of cases.

With this example, Valle attempts to diminish the sensational effect, working strenuously on maintaining consistency with the values of the surrounding city. This complex mechanism, proposed as a system of urban blocks in the city centre, is significant in showing how much an urban renewal project of such a size — almost seventy thousand square metres — can also express urban values and be integrated into the existing city.

The buildings are made with prefabricated reinforced-concrete elements, and express that pragmatic and sober character that identifies the architecture for the service and industrial sectors of Valle's "Friulan period." Projecting roofs and balconies positioned along the pedestrian streets help to give an urban character to the whole and, at the same time, guarantee a continuous covering along the shopping route, necessary for the functioning of a commercial "machine."

A timid attempt to introduce a kind of pluri-functionality occurs on the main entrance street from the city, where a multi-floor building houses offices and urban services on the upper floors and stores on the ground floor. Even so, we are still far from the European examples mentioned in this book, such as the Stadshart of Almere, the Debis in Potsdamer Platz, or Hamburg's HafenCity, where a structural hybrid corresponds to a hybrid of functions and uses, between the commercial ground floor and the residential and service upper floors — examples of a fruitful re-creation of true urban vitality, besides variety of form.

Formal variety, in the relative homogeneity of functions, was also sought after in a rather fierce way by C. Zucchi, who instilled a landscape dimension, both in morphology and architectural language, into the planimetric/volumetric design inherited from Valle. Starting from the outlines identified in the urban plan, Zucchi introduces a free sequence of towers representing an interpretation of the combination approach already tested by Valle in his shopping complex. And thus, in a significant way, he harmonizes the entrance to the urban park, the centre of the new part of the city. A collage of building types, Zucchi's city block mirrors in a vaguely functionalist way the categories of residential uses: renovation construction, subsidized housing, the re-use of the former Alfa Romeo cafeteria as a residence-service facility. And so, while the row buildings mark, with a solid stone base, the city block along the via Traiano, the towers dissolve into a pointillist powder of balconies, glass panels, metal parapets, and backgrounds of variously coloured plaster, communicating with the sinuosity of the park by C. Jencks and A. Kipar, which they overlook. This park is a garden of "hills" that follows the morphology and shape of the artificial Mount Stella (a small hill with surrounding park designed by Piero Bottoni in the aftermath of the Second World War) as well as the pre-Alpine elevations in the distance, which can ideally be seen on clear days from the higher floors of the buildings. Transcribed as a work of land art, using the dug-up earth from the underground parking lots, the park is built in a fluid sequence of concave-convex shapes in mutual reflection: subservient to the dominant spiral geometry, the empty space of the lake materializes in the fullness of the vortex of the promontory-belvedere.

Even the superblock planned by Studio Canali attempts to respond to the place's two strong presences: the city to the north and the new park to the south. The curtain-style construction allows for the acquiring of a large semi-public park, an interface between city and park and a place to accommodate a sequence of towers evoking Frank Lloyd Wright, both for its explicit architectural references and for its tendency to organically mix "artifice and nature."

The landscape breakdown also guided Valle towards a morphological configuration of the square with the three buildings of the service sector positioned on the edge of the Fiera Milano City. Valle responds to the difficult situation of relating to the overflow gable, designed by M. Bellini in the 1980s as a monumental end to the exhibition pavilions, with a delicate work of deconstruction – namely, three semi-gables freely relocated on the ground. In the formulation of the whole, they acquire a geographical role, with the large unified parterre garden designed by Topotek, capable of serving as a counterbalance to the park beyond the boulevard, to which it reunites with an agile leap towards the cable-stayed projecting canopy achieved by Arup.

**Milan**, Nuova Portello

Urban planning: Studio Valle Architetti Associati
Strategic coordination: Ennio Brion
General coordination: Pirelli RE
Landscape planning: Charles Jencks, Andreas Kipar-Land
Development company: Ennio Brion-Nuova Portello, Auredia
Planning and implementation: 2002–ongoing

1 Shopping Centre: Studio Valle Architetti Associati
2 Park: C. Jencks: A. Kipar-Land
3 Residences northwest block: Cino Zucchi Architetti
4 Residences northeast block: Canali Associati
5 Kindergarten: Canali Associati
6 Offices southeast bay: Studio Valle Architetti Associati
7 Square southeast bay: Topotek
8 Cyclo-pedestrian Boardwalk: Arup Italia

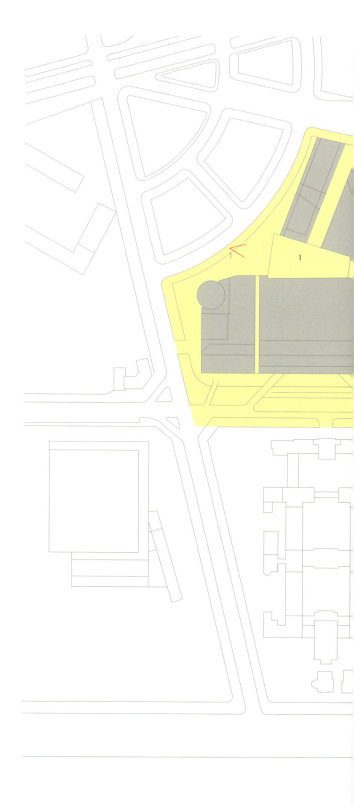

3

# Paris, Parc Bercy, Seine Rive Gauche

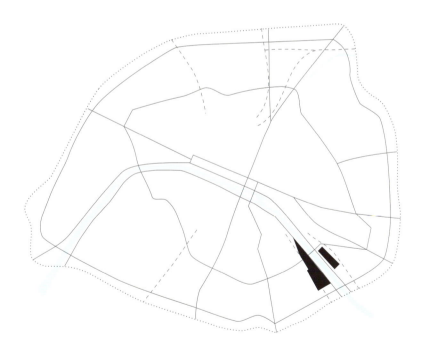

Towards the end of the 1970s, when Paris became aware of the empty sites to the east of the city, new practices in urban construction were coming to the fore on the contemporary architectural horizon. The need for a profound revision of methods and principles in project development began to take hold. It was necessary to counter the model of a metropolis dissolving into the territory set aside for *grands ensembles*.

The Plan d'occupation du sol of 1974 had already projected a change in intentions in urban transformation practices. After a careful study of the city fabric, Atelier parisien d'urbanisme (APUR), outlined an approach to urban renewal, distinguishing areas for *rénovation* from those of *restauration*. Returning to the street alignment, the limits in terms of height, and the partitioning for city blocks reveals the new intentions emerging out of the research on the historic city, and heralding the appearance of a *nouvelle vague* in town planning.

The "re-conquest" of the Parisian east encouraged by the motto "Paris se lève à l'est" (Paris rises in the east), initiates this course shift: the urgency in reviving the obsolete areas, which had been abandoned during the industry closures, and in reorganizing the rail configuration steers the expansion process of the centre – in other words, the extension of its physical and spatial elements. Adopted in 1983 by the municipality, governed then by Jacques Chirac, the Plan Programme de l'est de Paris incorporates different renewal practices within a general strategy of urban policy, tending to improve the value of this part of the city. The tools and methods for implementation are well-known and already tested: the procedure for the implementation of the urban plan of the Zones d'aménagement concerté (ZAC) allows for the interweaving of negotiation practices, saving it from the rigidity of the plan, while Société d'économie mixte (SEM) constitutes the operative and economic arm that allows the public service provider to assume the control of urban transformation.

In the desire to produce *morceaux de ville* – city segments able to take on the spatiality and high density of the centre – distance is taken from both the zoning practices for *grands ensembles* carried out by the previous plan and the practices of architectural spectacle wished for by François Mitterrand. The policies of the mayor enters into competition with the projects of the president, sealing not so much an institutional conflict but more the contrast between two different urban ideas. One idea in the wake of the theories of the Eighth International Congress of Modern Architecture, "the heart of the city," celebrates the symbol of collective representation in the block monument, symbolically relaunching the demands for renewal of the city. The other, recalling the lesson of Haussmann, revolves around the public space with its high quality features in order to bestow an urban identity to the extensive suburbs. Between such polarities, we have the presidential *Grands Projets* on the one hand and, on the other, the more delicate work of the *aménagement*, promoted by the Parisian municipality with fifty or more ZAC.

This was a polarity of position that eventually exhausted itself, and the two urban policies and the two cultural options have effectively become fused together. The architectural renewal, pursued by Mitterrand's political-cultural program and produced through the "exceptionality" of the new cutting-edge planning themes, was in fact transferred onto projects of urban transformation, arriving at interesting combinations, as in ZAC de Bercy and ZAC Seine Rive Gauche (renamed Paris Rive Gauche in 1996).

Unlike most abandoned industrial sites, the large area of the wine warehouses in Bercy had outstanding settlement and environmental qualities even before the renewal. Aligned on perpendicular paved streets following the course of the Seine River, warehouses and buildings of a certain merit from the end of the nineteenth century were inserted among over five hundred centuries-old trees, the legacy of the eighteenth-century gardens of Bercy, the old holiday resort of the Parisian nobility. These exceptional environmental qualities have been enhanced by the new morphological configuration, dominated by the large park.

Like its adopted reference models, including London squares and the monumental spaces of the Parisian centre, Parc Bercy plays a passive strategic role in the Parisian urban layout. It does not oversee the settlement principles of the surrounding buildings and infrastructures, but, a posteriori, it succeeds in marking out connections, thus giving meaning to the revitalization works as they expand and gradually move towards the edges of the plan's geographical boundaries, which were without formal definition for years. In the competition design, Huet and Ferrand, winners of the 1987 international consultation, express the will to reunite and reposition the fragmentary building and infrastructure works, which had been situated on the edges of the park by chance and without any sense of coordination With the rigid urban structure of the neo-Haussmann approach of APUR abandoned, the park seems to make sense, starting from a precise interpretation of the remnants of the old fabric of the warehouses. With archaeological patience, the oblique and irregular trails of the descent towards the Seine become restored, thus highlighting the existing rows of centuries-old trees and the remaining building fragments. A new weave of routes is superimposed onto the trails that run parallel to the rediscovered streets.

Three different types of gardens in sequence – *la prairie, les parterres, le jardin romantique* – relate the Palais Omnisports to Bercy Village. The gardens look out onto the Seine with a long terrace rising up from an articulated infrastructure that accommodates parking areas and service facilities in the spaces beneath. A solid defensive barrier against the express road coming from the Boulevard périphérique, the terrace, however, blocks the park's connection to the Seine.

A well-chosen integration, Huet Park joins up with the park thoroughfare to the east and is designed by Hammoutène, Chaix, Morel, Montes, Lion, Dusapin, Leclercq, de Portzamparc, and Ciriani, with Buffi's coordination and the end of the park designed by Gehry. The park thoroughfare of Bercy is born out of a coordinated plan, connecting the morphological layout of the whole with the individual buildings, without availing itself of regulatory coercive systems. Urban building principles, freely acquired from the architects, are reinterpreted in the sharing of a "common culture" around the modern architecture of the city. Along the frontage of six hundred metres facing onto the park, gaps open out between the garden and the city at its back. Such is the new environmental situation that it demands research into specific and appropriate designs for the city block model – a city block to rethink the complexity of its forms, and not simply deduced from urban conventions. New rules of *découpage* arrange the connections within and outside the city block and those between the various blocks. Each planner is entrusted with portions of a block and an urban space rather than "building plots." The methodical process surrounding the block produces a fragmentation of the parts and their subsequent descent, so that the park frontage can collect itself into a whole: a divisionist fade-out of the elements, one that is sensitive to the qualities of light and air, is contrasted with the environmental and plant enclosure that it faces.

When ZAC Bercy was already under construction, Paris, compressed between the waters of the Seine and the railroad tracks of the Gare d'Austerlitz, still gave the impression of an enormous railway enclave: an industrial suburban landscape between the Boulevard périphérique and the Jardin des Plantes, two kilometres from Notre-Dame. In 1992, the municipality, along with the SNCF, launched the urban renewal project based on the example of Parc Bercy beyond the Seine. But here it was not the park that suggested the morphology of the new neighbourhood. An uninterrupted *dalle* (esplanade), a new artificial base, passes over the clusters of train tracks to make some space for the city. The different relationship that it establishes with the city and the infrastructure distances it from the city as machine model, which had been tested in the Défense business district in the 1960s with controversial results.

A new system of proportions ties what is below ground to what is above ground. With the rail yard near the Seine dismantled, a new urban district rises above the quays and the surrounding city. The Avenue de France, axis of the new development, runs ten metres higher than the railway bed upon which support structures are arranged between the tracks, supporting the platform and the whole of the foundation for the buildings above. The Austerlitz district, based on a plan of Ch. Devillers, reworked into the morphology of streets and blocks, wedges itself right into the city. R. Schweitzer creates the Tolbiac Nord district around the Bibliothèque Mitterrand by D. Perrault as a symbolic centre of the development and a landmark for all Paris. In the Masséna Nord neighbourhood that reaches to the edge of the Boulevard périphérique, Ch. de Portzamparc fuses the street alignments of a truly urban model with a cluster-type structure located in the internal gardens. B. Fortier, in the Masséna Chevaleret neighbourhood, arranges a system of urban blocks between the surrounding city and the underlying tracks.

Routinely within a coordinated urban project, different planners in separate projects identify the morphological layout and the guidelines for the many architects that become involved. Blocks and single buildings, although they follow the dictates of urban conventions, are created according to contemporary styles and with contemporary materials, and cross-referenced with the Bibliothèque Mitterrand. Building textures, metal or wood grilles, and glass panelling relate to each other in a visible and perceptible elegance, reflecting the environmental qualities of the site – light, water, and vegetation. Passageways and glass walls open out onto visible destinations and transparencies, destabilizing and, at the same time, enriching the conventional morphological models. The infrastructures, neither completely obliterated nor intensely highlighted, but in harmony with the city, participate in the fullest type of urban enjoyment by being partially visible to the overlooking urban spaces.

Together with other contemporary experiments, the Avenue Wilson by M. Corajoud, covering the A1 in the Plaine Saint-Denis and the Gare de Montparnasse with the overlooking Penà Gardens, represents a good example of covering for large transit infrastructures. Laid out on new "ground" rather than suspended on a "slab," this comforting sloping of a hanging city mixes urban character, landscape, and infrastructures, providing richness and variety as well as original qualitative values to a section of the compact city.

Parc Bercy and Seine Rive Gauche are among the most significant episodes in the renewal of the Parisian eastside. With the two areas as objects of separate and independent urban renewal works, an overall vision of the urban section situated between the two abandoned railway yards was lost and the connection to the Seine as well as a possible connection between the two banks was sacrificed.

Two adjacent districts around Parc Bercy and centering on the Bibliothèque Mitterrand have been built up relatively independently. The angular towers of the Bibliothèque that we see sprouting from Parc Bercy and from the elegant Passerelle (walkway) Simone-de-Beauvoir allow for the predicting of the possibilities of a design attentive to the Seine and its quays, and ready to assign to them an important role in the configuration of the whole. In the first reflections formulated for Expo '89, some organic plans amply illustrate the advantages offered by a design with a "crossing over" of the Seine – virtues exceedingly evident in the layout of certain monumental spaces of the city.

**Paris**, Parc Bercy, Seine Rive Gauche

*Parc Bercy*
Urban planning: Atelier Parisien d'Urbanisme (APUR)
Coordination of the Fronteparco: Jean Pierre Buffi
Plan of Parc Bercy: B. Huet, M. Ferrand, J. Feugas, B. Le Roy
Development company: Semest–ZAC Bercy
Planning and implementation: 1989–1995

*Seine Rive Gauche*
Urban planning and coordination: Christian Devillers (Austerlitz Nord), Roland Schweitzer (Tolbiac Nord), Christian de Portzamparc, Ateliers Lion (Masséna Nord), Bruno Fortier, Jean-Thierry Bloch, Ateliers Lion (Masséna Chevaleret)

Development company: Semapa
Planning and implementation: 1988–ongoing

1 Cinémathèque Française: F. Gehry
2 Residence: F. Hammoutène
3 Residence: Chaix & Morel
4 Residence: F. Montes
5 Residence: Y. Lion
6 Residence: Dusapin & Leclercq
7 Residence: C. de Portzamparc
8 Residence: H. Ciriani
9 Parc Bercy: B. Huet, M. Ferrand, J. Feugas, B. Le Roy, I. Le Caisne, P. Raguin
10 Bercy Village: Valode & Pistre
11 Ministère de l'Economie: Chemetov & Huidobro
12 Palais Omnisports: Andrault & Parat
13 Boardwalk Simone de Beauvoir: D. Feichtinger
14 Caisse des Dépôts et Consignations: C. Hauvette
15 BPCE: Jodry & Turner
16 Le Fulton: Valode & Pistre
17 Residence: J. Roca
18 Offices: Chaix & Morel
19 Residence: P. Gangnet
20 Residence: F. Hammoutène
21 Equinoxe: Thin & Cianfaglione, P. Gravereaux
22 Bibliothèque François Mitterrand: D. Perrault
23 MK2: Namur & Wilmotte
24 Residence: F. Soler
25 Athos: J. Charpentier
26 Offices: Dusapin & Leclercq
27 Residence: R. Bofill, Giraud & Hecly
28 Residence: Brenac & Gonzales
29 Residence: E. Girard
30 Offices: A. Grumbach
31 Residence: C. Furet
32 Residence: J. Pargade
33 Residence: C. Devillers
34 Residence: A. Stinco
35 Grands Moulins Université Paris 7: R. Ricciotti
36 Esplanade des Grands Moulins: Interscène Paysagistes
37 Banque Populaire: C. Devillers
38 Residence: H. Gaudin
39 Université Paris 7: Chaix & Morel
40 Ministère de la Jeunesse et des Sports: J. Viguier
41 Residence: Brenac & Gonzales
42 Département-Ville de Paris: Chementov & Huidobro
43 Jardin Cyprien-Norwid: Atelier Tournesol

15
16

# Saint-Denis, Plaine Saint-Denis

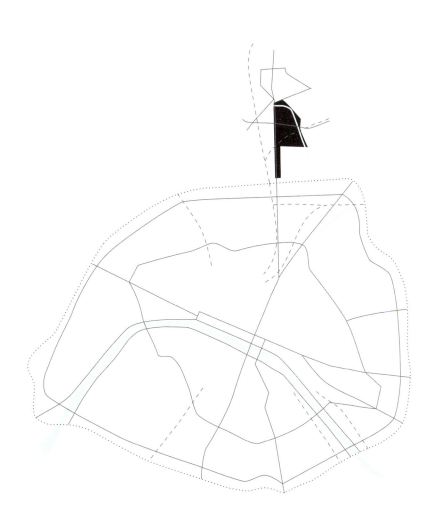

Holding to landscape principles, an ambitious urban project has regenerated the large territory north of Paris that stretches over seven hundred hectares between the Boulevard périphérique and the Cathedral of Saint-Denis: the Plaine Saint-Denis. The metropolitan conurbation that has risen here has seen a chaotic stratification of functions and infrastructures over the years. The nineteenth century located chemical and manufacturing industries here due to the presence of rail yards and the navigable canal of Saint-Denis. In the twentieth century, this canal was the primary infrastructure for the greatly trafficked connection between the north of France and the capital. Ultimately, in the 1960s, the large residential complexes would densify the entire zone of towns between Paris and the new cities, further bringing congestion to the already immense Parisian suburbs.

Plaine Saint-Denis is a broad-ranging project that fractures the borders between city and infrastructure, city and landscape, and urban and landscape projects. With the conventional rules of urban construction in disorder, the experiments conducted here completely seal the old divisions. The landscape/city, man-made/natural dichotomy that still informs heroic modernism dissolve into a coexistence of multiple elements that make way for complex and stratified settlement fusions. However, current urban planning practices seem to be founded on and confused with landscape planning. On the Plaine Saint-Denis, the construction of a city together with landscape has been patiently proposed, both working in a commonality of materials and techniques. The simultaneous manipulation of building, vegetation, infrastructure, and geography without building according to an a priori poetic or stylistic principle, in fact, becomes the working principle that allows for the employment of an effective transformation and improvement of the existing reality.

*Terrain vague*, heterotopic spaces, underutilized infrastructures, remnants of manufacturing closures – no longer features to eliminate – are rather landscape fragments that create the heterogeneous richness of the contemporary city. In these circumstances, the group of architects and landscape designers known as Hippodamos 93 (Y. Lion, M. Corajoud, P. Riboulet, and P. Robert) at the beginning of the 1990s formulated three principles for qualitative transformation and environmental restoration: "to improve the landscape elements present on the site," "to establish with resolve the public space," and "to graft an economic plan onto the urban plan" (Corajoud 1994).

What M. Corajoud defines as the *horizons-paysages* are those landscape singularities of a place that links the hill of Montmartre, the Basilica of Saint-Denis, and the geography of the Seine. Here we have a new conception predicated on the landscape. This conception is original both in perceptual terms and functionality, and provides great appeal. The landscape refers to the important evidence of the industrial history – the wide horizons on the rail yards, the curves of the railway lines and of the bays of the canals, the infrastructure imprints and objects. This "full recovery" approach is best. It capitalizes on the conflicting stratifications deposited over time, rather than condemning them to obliteration in the name of the pre-existing natural landscape to be revived or in the name of purely aesthetic works of camouflage. Artificial, certainly, but it is what this landscape is. Besides, one does not respond to the necessity of "establishing a public space" through conventional notions of urban space. Thorough research finds new ways of envisaging open spaces: it rediscovers intersections, sees novel connections in the old, mixes plant elements with pavement, structures with infrastructures. Set against a principle of hierarchical structuring of urban spaces and infrastructures is a "rhizomatic" and pervasive vision, which drives the new open spaces to insinuate themselves between the interstices of the development and to destabilize the usual division of public, semi-public, and private. A new geography, built through inclusions and adjustments, is produced based on a principle that governs subsequent approximations in an ongoing process, more than on the determination to finish a prearranged project on time. This is a principle that allows for the accommodation of ongoing projects and opportunities like the new Stade de France for the 1998 World Cup or the Olympic village that was envisaged here after the Paris application for the Olympic Games.

The ambition of the mayor of Saint-Denis, Patrick Braouezec, who launched the development involving the bordering municipalities, has been to merge an economic plan with an urban plan. He desired an economic and social renewal of the local communities by elevating the environmental quality of a large swath of intercommunal territory. The landscape operation, intended to provide greater functionality and quality to the spaces, links sections that were functionally and physically separate within a new interconnecting network, thus bestowing a new image upon the city in order to attract investors and new inhabitants. Thirteen ZAC have been inaugurated, even though until now it does not seem as if the quality of planning and implementation anticipated by the Hippodamos group has prevailed. Certain realities, however, stand out in the thoroughness and abundance of the renewal works: the Avenue Wilson obtained by covering a section of the highway A1, the new city section centering on the Avenue du Stade de France, the navigable Canal Saint-Denis recovered and phased into the networks dedicated for collective use, and the Plaine de la Plaine.

Michel Corajoud and the Hippodamos 93 team consider the covering of Highway A1 the essential condition for executing the urban and environmental regeneration for this section of the territory. This operation acquires a demonstrative value: a landscape project has to trigger transformative processes, rehabilitate, and rectify, not only smooth out contradictions by concealing them with a cover-up of "green" works. "Rehabilitating as in the case of war damage, territorial expropriation, and urban devastation" was undertaken in 1960 (Corajoud 1994). They got rid of the old royal axis road, which, with a monumental planting of chestnut trees, used to connect the Basilica of Saint-Denis with Notre Dame, in order to sink the highway, which from the Boulevard périphérique crosses the residential districts to the northeast. It is of no use to mitigate the monstrous effects of this with "gift-wrapping of greenery," as Alain Roger calls the decorative works appended to the wounds inflicted on the landscape. Instead, it is necesary to offer new functions, to produce new physical and spatial relationships with "structural" modifications capable of interconnecting the divided city sections. Already proposed at the end of the 1960s, the covering could only be implemented thanks to the investments that came about as a result of the 1998 World Cup for the construction of the Stade de France on the land north of the Plaine. As a centre of a new neighbourhood accomplished via the ZAC method, with hotels, offices, entertainment venues, and homes, the new stadium and the investments it inspired have provided a decisive stimulus for the launching of rehabilitation works already anticipated in the urban and landscape plan for the Plaine.

Built in 1999 by landscape architect Corajoud, the lighting designer Fashard for the illumination, and the architect Lion for the building segments, the covering is configured like a *dalle* (esplanade) of around five hectares, a kilometre and a half long. It organizes the planted gardens one after the other, the parterre gardens with rest and play areas, and the spaces for local and small provision markets for use by the neighbourhood. Somewhere between an artificial garden and an urban infrastructure, the structure, supported by perpendicular trusses on the highway route, functions, with its limited width, as an osmotic barrier between the city above and the transit tunnel beneath. Two non-compatible worlds occasionally interact: ventilation grilles, wells with glass floors, and windows resurface in the linear garden above, integrating into the design of the planted parterre gardens and that of the pavement. Two tree-lined service roads follow these routes, interrupted by the highway trench, and re-establish the network and the transit and pedestrian connection between the different neighbourhoods. Small buildings function as entrances to the different parts of the garden: visible signposts from the revived urban outline highlight the presence in the distance of this new "centre crosspiece" that invigorates the entire development.

Formulated by the French group Mosbach Paysagistes, the project for the renewal of the shores of the Canal Saint-Denis in 2000 alters and enhances the routes and the areas that overlook the east bank. Built in Napoleonic times to bring the waters of the Villette basin to the Seine, Canal Saint-Denis presents the homogeneity of a paleo-industrial infrastructure. By means of the inclusion of residue materials, left over from the activities established in different eras, the renewal works rediscover new connections between the settlements and the canal, and spatially express the interference of various local situations with the geographic scale of the infrastructure. A walk reveals in sequence the features of the industrial periphery, the locks, the silos, the swing bridges, all recovered as parts of a new inclusive landscape. A green belt continues for seven kilometres, parallel to the course of the water; between the city and the canal, a *banquette végétale* with various plants accompanies the route, interrupted only in correspondence to the locks. Different clusters of routes articulate the walk: a stripe of rough cement *désactivé* marks the access road for service vehicles, while the cycle path is made of smooth concrete. Within the green border, diversely articulated paths and different rest areas are enriched by various plantings and pavements and by the relationship with the surrounding territory. The colours along the canal, repeated and presented again with materials, road signs, general signage, and vegetation, tend to reinforce the unified character of the walk and, at the same time, articulate it with respect to the specific features of the surroundings.

**Saint-Denis**, Plaine Saint-Denis

Urban and Landscape Planning:
SEM PCD, Hippodamos 93 – M. Corajoud, P. Riboulet, Y. Lion, P. Robert
Development company: SEM Plaine Commune Développement
Planning and implementation: 1992–2002

1 Avenue Wilson: M. Corajoud, P. Riboulet, Y. Lion, P. Robert
2 Promenade Canal Saint-Denis: Mosbach Paysagistes
3 Stade de France: Macary, Zubléna, Costantini, Regembal
4 ZAC du Cornillon Nord
5 Canal Saint-Denis

# Bibliography

Auctores varii (various authors). 1985. *La ricostruzione della Città*. Milan: Electa.
- 1986. *Progetto Bicocca*. Milan: Electa.
- 1987. *Architectures Capitales, Paris 1979–1989*. Paris: Electa Moniteur.
- 1987. "Internationale Bauausstellung Berlin. Die Neubaugebiete. Dokumente-Projekte1984/87." Berlin: IBA
- 1990. *Barcelona Arquitectura y Ciudad 1980–1992*. Barcelona: Gustavo Gili.
- 1994. *I racconti dell'abitare*. Milan: Segesta, Milan Triennale.
- 1994. "La Ville." In *Art et architecture en Europe 1870–1993*. Paris: Centre Pompidou.
- 1994. *La Ville*. Paris: Le Moniteur.
- 1995. *Il Centro altrove*. Milan: Milan Triennale, Electa.
- 1995. *Nove parchi per Milano*. Milan: Electa.
- 1995. *Progetto Bicocca*. Milan: Milan Triennale, Electa.
- 1996. *The Compact City. A Sustainable Urban Form*. London: E & FN Spon.
- 1999. "I Quaderni delle Bicocca 01." Milan: Skira.
- 2001. *Mutations*. Barcelona: Actar.
- 2001. *Harvard Design School Guide to Shopping*. Cologne: Taschen.
- 2002. *New Netherlands Architecture*. Rotterdam: Nai Publishers. *Projets Urbains en France*. Paris: Le moniteur.
- 2003. *Eastern Docklands Amsterdam*. Amsterdam: Arcam.
- 2003. *Inside Density*. Paris: La lettre volée.
- 2003. *Penser la ville par la Lumière*, Paris: Le Moniteur
- 2003. *Penser la ville par le Paysage*, Paris: Le Moniteur
- 2003. *Planning Amsterdam. Scenarios for Urban Development, 1928–2000*. Rotterdam: Nai Publishers.
- 2003. *Trasformazioni a Milano*. Milan: Franco Angeli.

Amidon, J. 2001. *Radical Landscapes*. London: Thames & Hudson.
Anderson, S., ed. 1978. *On Street*, Cambridge, MA: MIT Press.
Arendt, H. 1958. *Vita Activa*. Chicago: University of Chicago Press.
Augé, M. 1986. *Un ethnologue dans le metro*. Paris: Hachette.
- 1992. *Non lieux,*. Paris: Seuil.
- 1993. *Nonluoghi*. Milan: Elèuthera.
- 1997. *L'Impossible voyage. Le tourisme et ses images*. Paris: Payot & Rivages.
- Ayuntamento de Barcelona. 1986. "Plan Especial de la Zona Costera Metropolitana".
- 1987. "Plans Cap 92."

Bagnasco, A. 1994. *Fatti sociali formati nello spazio*. Milan: Franco Angeli.
Banham, R. 1971. *The Architecture of Four Ecologies*. New York: Penguin.
- 1983. *L'architettura della quattro ecologie*. Genoa: Costa & Nolan.
Benjamin, W. 2007. *I «passages» di Parigi*. Turin: Einaudi.
Berman, M. 1982. *The Experience of Modernity*. New York: Simon & Schuster.
- 1985. *L'esperienza della modernità*. Bologna: Il Mulino.
- 1991. "Immagini della metropoli modernista." In *Atlante metropolitano*. Milan: Electa.
Berque, A. 1995. *Les raison du paysage*. Paris: Hazan.
Bohigas, O. 1985. *Vila Olimpica: transformación de un frente marítimo*. Relazione di progetto.
- 1992. *Ricostruire Barcellona*. Milan: Etas Libri.
Bru, E. 1998. *New Landscape, New Territories*. Barcelona: Actar.
Busquets, J. 1992. *Barcelona*. Barcelona: Mapfre.
Calatrava, S. 1998. *Public Buildings*. Zurich: Birkhauser.
Calthorpe, P. 1993. *The Next American Metropolis: Ecology Community and the American Dream*. Princeton: Princeton Architectural Press.
Clément, G. 1999. *Le jardin en mouvement*. Paris: Sens et Tonka.
- 1999. *Le jardin planétaire*. Paris: Albin Michel.
Choay, F. 1992. *L'orizzonte del post urbano*. Rome: Officina edizioni.
Comune di Milano. 1983. "Progetto passante." General document.
Corajoud, M. 1994. *Plaine Saint Denis*. Project report.
Corboz, A. 1998. *Ordine sparso*. Milan: Franco Angeli.
Davis, M. 1990. *City of the Quarz*. London: Verso.
- 1993. *La città di quarzo*. Rome: Manifesto libri.
- 1998. *Ecology of Fear*. New York: Metropolitan Books.

– 1999. *Geografia della paura.* Milan: Feltrinelli.
Debord, G. 1967. *La societé du spectacle.* Paris: Buchet-Castel.
Deleuze, G., and F. Guattari. 1980. *Mille Plateaux: Capitalisme et schizophrenie.* Paris: Éditions de Minuit
– 2003. *Millepiani: capitalismo e schizofrenia.* Rome: Castelvecchi.
de Solà-Morales, I. 1983. "Arte civica contro città funzionale (di nuovo)." In *Lotus* 39.
– 1988. "La segunda historia del Proyecto Urbano." In *Urbanismo revista* 5, 6 .
– 1988. *Mnemosi o retorica: la crisi della rappresentazione nella città e nell'architettura moderna.* Milan: Electa.
– 1989. "Un'altra tradizione moderna." In *Lotus* 64.
– 2000. *Progettare Città.* Milan: Elemond.
– 2001. "Territori." In *Lotus* 110.
Devillers, C. 1994. *Le projet urbain.* Paris: Éditions du Pavillon de l'Arsenal.
Donadieu, P. 1994. *Cinq propositions pour une théorie du paysage.* Paris: Champ Vallon.
Ellin, N. 1999. *Postmodern Urbanis.* Princeton: Princeton University Press.
Forman, T., and M. Godron. 1986. *Landscape Ecology.* New York: Wiley & Sons.
Foucault, M. 1994. *Eterotopia, Luoghi e non luoghi metropolitani.* Milan: Mimesis.
Gans, H. 1962. *The Urban Villagers.* New York: Free Press.
Goffman, E. 1997. *La vita quotidiana come rappresentazione.* Bologna: Il mulino.
Grumbach, A. "Les promenades de Paris." In *L'architecture d'aujoud'hui* 185.
HafenCity Hamburg. 2009. *The Birth of the City.* Hamburg: HafenCity Gmbh.
– 2011. *Projekte.* Hamburg: HafenCity Gmbh.
Hall, P. 1973. *Planning and Urban Growth: An Anglo-American Comparison.* Baltimore: Johns Hopkins University Press.
– 1996. *Cities of Tomorrow.* London: Blackwell.
Hannerz, U. 1992. *Esplorare la Città. Antropologia della vita urbana.* Bologna: Il Mulino.
Harwey, D. 1989. *The Urban Experience.* London: Blackwell.
– 1990. *The Condition of Postmodernity.* London: Blackwell.
– 1993. *La crisi della modernità.* Milan: Il saggiatore.
Hucliez, M. 1999. *Jardins et parcs contemporains.* Paris: Telleri.
Ingallina, P. 2001. *Projet Urbain.* Paris: PUF.
Ingallina, P., and M. Roncayolo. 2000. *Dictionnaire de l'urbanisme et de l'amenagement.* Paris: PUF.
Ingersoll, R. 2004. *Sprawltown.* Rome: Meltemi.
Jacobs, J. 1961. *The Death and Life of Great American Cities.* New York: Random House.
– 1969. *Vita e morte delle grandi città.* Turin: Einaudi.
Jameson, J. 1984. "Postmodernism, Or the Cultural Logic of Late Capitalism." *New Left Review* 1(146).
Koolhaas, R. 1978. *Delirius New York.* New York: Monacelli Press.
– 1988. *Euralille.* Project report.
– 1997. "La Città generica." In *Domus* 791.
Koolhaas R., and B. Mau. 1995. *S, M, L, XL.* New York: Monacelli Press.
Lyotard, F. 1979. *La Condition postmoderne: Rapport sur le savoir.* Paris: Les Éditions de Minuit.
Marinoni, G. 2005. *Metamorfosi del progetto urbano.* Milan: Franco Angeli.
– 2006. *Infrastrutture nel progetto urbano.* Milan: Franco Angeli.
– 2009. "Mediation of the City." In *Lotus* 139.
– 2012. *Urban Landscape Strategies.* Milan: SMOwnPublishing.
Martinotti, G. 1993. *Metropoli: la nuova morfologia sociale della città.* Bologna: Il Mulino.
Massey, D. 1984. *Spatial Divisions of Labour: Social Structures and the Geography of Production.* London: Macmillan.
Mazza, L. 1993. "Conservazione e trasformazione: una ridefinizione del piano regolatore." In *Controspazio* 5.
– 1997. *Trasformazioni del piano.* Milan: Franco Angeli.
Mazza, L., ed. 1988. *Le città del mondo e il futuro della metropoli.* Milan: Milan Triennale, Electa.
Mostafavi, M., and G. Doherty. 2010. *Ecological Urbanism.* Baden: Lars Muller Publishers.
Nicolin, P. 1998. *Elementi di architettura.* Milan: Skira.
Nicolin P., ed. 1987. *Le città immaginate. Viaggio in Italia, Nove progetti per Nove città.* Milan: Milan Triennale, Electa.
– 1991. *Atlante metropolitano.* Milan: Electa.
Nicolin P., G. Marinoni, and A. Rocca, eds. 1992. *Metamorfosi dell'architettura urbana.* Milan: Electa.
Panerai, P., J. Castex, and J. Depaule. 1980. *Isolato urbano e città contemporanea.* Milan: Clup.
Piano, R. 1995. *Opera complete.* Turin: Allemandi & C.
Piattelli Palmarini, M. 1985. *L'illusione di sapere.* Milan: Mondadori.
– 1987. *Livelli di realtà.* Milan: Feltrinelli.
Rogier, A. 1997. *Court traité du Paysage.* Paris: Edition Gallimard.
Roncayolo, M. *La ville aujourd'hui.* Paris: Editions du Seuil.
Rowe, C., and F. Koetter. 1978. *Collage City.* Milan: Il Saggiatore.
Simon, M. 1995. *Arret sur images.* Lille: EuraLille.
Sorkin, M. 1992. *Variations on a Theme Park.* New York: Hill and Wang.
– 2003. "Pensieri sulla densità." In *Lotus* 117.
Teyssot, G. 1988. "Il 'teatro' della metropoli: conclusioni e interrogative." In *Atlante metropolitano.* Milan: Electa.
– 2000. "Lo spazio pubblico e il fantasma dell'agorà." In *Lotus* 106.
Town Planning Department. 2003. "City Renewal and the Region." Exhibition, City of Amsterdam.
Urry, J. 2000. *Lo sguardo del turista.* Formello: Edizioni Seam.

*Magazines and Periodicals Consulted with Issue Numbers*
*a+t,* 19, 20, 25
*A+U,* 329, 352
*Abitare,* 394, 402, 417, 453
*Almere perspectief,* 3
*The Architectural Record,* 3
*The Architectural Review,* 1112, 1146, 1158, 1174, 1189, 1223, 1235
*Architektur + Wettbewerbe,* 150, 158
*Area,* 37, 42, 66, 76
*Arquitectura y Critica,* 46, 49, 52
*Casabella,* 487–8, 501, 524, 553–4, 575–6, 585, 597–8, 600, 606, 615, 616, 617, 623, 626, 628–9, 630, 656, 678
*Chassé park Bericht,* 3, 5, 6, 11
*Domus,* 791, 815, 834, 839, 844, 866, 877
*El Croquis,* 53, 67, 79, 111, 113, 115
*Het stucturplan,* 2–3, 4–5
*Jaarverslag,* 2
*L'architecture d'aujoud'hui,* 242, 280, 295, 296, 297, 298, 350
*Le Moniteur,* 19, 55, 67
*Les Annales de la recherche urbaine,* 51, 82, 88, 90
*Lotus,* 64, 67, 69, 71, 80, 84, 86, 87, 88, 94, 96, 99, 109, 110, 117, 122, 123, 131, 139
*Navigator,* 2, 5, 7, 8, 9
*Pages Paysages,* 6, 8
*Paris projet,* 12, 13, 15, 16, 18
*Parametro,* 256
*Projet urbain,* 11, 15, 17
*Quaderns,* 240, 245, 246
*Rassegna,* 18, 36, 37, 42, 54, 75
*Stadchart Journal,* 4, 6
*T&C,* 7, 9, 11
*Techniques & Architecture,* 395, 402, 403, 412, 421, 424, 432, 468, 471
*Topos,* 22, 33, 34, 37, 38, 44, 53, 55, 57
*Urbanisme,* 168–9
*Urbanistica,* 105, 120, 134
*Urbanismo revista,* 2, 5, 6
*Zodiac,* 18